The Open University

Educational Studies: A Third Level Course

E321 Management in Education

Unit 3

Schools as Organizations

Prepared by Digby Davies for the Course Team

The Open University Press

Course Team

Carolyn Baxter
Oliver Boyd-Barrett
Lydia Campbell
Sheila Dale
Digby Davies
Lance Dobson
Tony Gear (co-chairman)
Philip Healy
Donald Holms
Vincent Houghton (co-chairman)
Christine King
Royston McHugh
Reg Melton
John Miller
Edward Milner
Colin Morgan
Robert Nicodemus
Gerald Normie
Maggie Preedy
Gwynn Pritchard
Adam Westoby
Heather Young

The Open University Press
Walton Hall, Milton Keynes
MK7 6AA

First published 1976
Copyright © 1976 The Open University

Designed by the Media Development Group of the Open University.

Printed in Great Britain by
EYRE AND SPOTTISWOODE LIMITED
AT GROSVENOR PRESS, PORTSMOUTH

ISBN 0 335 06601 1

This text forms part of an Open University course. The complete list of units in the course appears at the end of this text.

For general availability of supporting material referred to in this text, please write to the Director of Marketing, The Open University, P.O. Box 81, Walton Hall, Milton Keynes, MK7 6AT.

Further information on Open University courses may be obtained from the Admissions Office, The Open University, P.O. Box 48, Walton Hall, Milton Keynes, MK7 6AB.

1.1

PREFACE

Unit 1 defined management, and compared management in education with management in other contexts. It also introduced some important themes in organization theory. We shall now develop these themes, focusing on schools as organizations. The major aims of Unit 3 are to provide a critical introduction to some main lines of organization theory and to examine their relevance to the management of schools.

As in Unit 1 we cover a wide field and the same reservations apply. Similarly, this unit is meant to serve the double function of standing both in its own right as a treatment of some central issues in educational management and as a backdrop to later units of the course.

Although no radio or television broadcasts are associated directly with this unit, many of the points raised here are relevant to the broadcasts, for example, those on the Sidney Stringer School and Community College.

OBJECTIVES

The unit is aimed at enabling the student to:

(a) Understand and discuss critically some main approaches to the organizational study of schools;

(b) Form a view on how organization theory and research relate to the management of schools;

(c) Acquire a range of concepts and models to describe and analyse schools and other educational organizations.

NOTES ON READING

Set reading

The following articles in Houghton, V. P., McHugh, G. A. R., and Morgan, C. (eds.) (1975) *Management in Education Reader 1: The Management of Organizations and Individuals*, London, Ward Lock Educational/The Open University Press:

(a) Hoyle, Eric 'The Study of Schools as Organizations' (Reading 2.2, pp. 85–108);

(b) Oldham, Joyce 'Organizational Analysis in Education: An Empirical Study of a School' (Reading 4.6, pp. 366–80);

(c) Greenfield, T. Barr 'Theory about Organization: A New Perspective and its Implications for Schools' (Reading 2.1, pp. 59–84).

These articles form the major reading for this unit and should be studied at the points indicated in the text.

In addition you will be referred to the set book: Hicks, H. G. (1967) *The Management of Organizations: A Systems and Human Resources Approach*, (2nd edn., 1972) New York, McGraw-Hill; and to other articles in *Reader 1* and in Dobson, L., Gear, T., and Westoby, A., (eds.) (1975) *Management in Education Reader 2: Some Techniques and Systems*, London, Ward Lock Educational/ The Open University Press.

Full references for further study are given at the end of the unit.

3

Recommended reading

If the subject of this unit is entirely new to you and you have time to do some preliminary reading then you may find the following books useful:

Bennett, S. J. (1974) *The School: An Organizational Analysis*, Glasgow, Blackie & Son Ltd.
Dunkerley, D. (1972) *The Study of Organizations*, London, Routledge & Kegan Paul Ltd.

No preliminary reading, however, is essential.

TIMING

The correspondence material for this unit contains the correspondence text and a series of student activities. In addition you will need to allow time for the reader articles and the set book. The times given below are only estimates. In practice, individuals will vary very much in the times they take over different portions of the unit. Please do not feel that you must adhere to the estimated times, but treat them as a guide to the way you distribute your time across the different parts of the unit.

Time schedule	hrs	mins
Correspondence text	4	00
Student activities	4	30
Reader articles and set book	4	00
Total	12	30

AUTHOR'S ACKNOWLEDGEMENT

The author wishes to express his gratitude to Harry Gray for his contribution to this unit. The help of Dr J. L. Dobson, a member of the E321 Course Team, with the historical note, paragraph 3.3, is also gratefully acknowledged.

CONTENTS

5

1 INTRODUCTION

1.1 Schools, along with industrial firms, army platoons, prisons and ballet-troupes, are organizations. The school as an organization moreover has a certain familiarity for all of us. As children we all attended school, and those of you who are teachers have current experience of the varieties of organizational arrangements and behaviour to be found in schools. The publicly perceived problems of schools are also familiar. They inhabit the media and everyday conversations. Schools are too formal, too informal, unwilling to innovate *and* over-eager to experiment. Schools fail to educate *and* fail to prepare students for jobs. Schools pay too much attention to social issues; they have not kept social issues out. The catalogue is both expandable *and* contradictory. These problems are 'organizational', in the sense of being attributed to 'schools', i.e. organizations, rather than to individuals. As such they are the concern of management. That is not to say that they are necessarily soluble or that only management should be concerned. It is, though, an assumption of recent training programmes for managers in education that a better understanding of schools as organizations can improve management performance in coping with such problems. Surveys of experienced teachers attending such programmes indicate a high acceptance of the value of organization theory for the practice of educational management.[1] A school may also have privately perceived problems which are more strictly 'organizational'. For instance, leadership may be seen by staff and students as too authoritarian or too weak. The school is too bureaucratic, or it lacks firm policy and rules. Consultation is inadequate or there are long, time-wasting meetings. Once more the list is potentially long and contradictory. These problems too are not necessarily capable of solution. There are no straightforward management techniques to apply as with, say, planning a timetable or controlling a budget. Nor are there agreed criteria for success. Again the assumption is that a better understanding of schools as organizations will lead to improved performances by heads and others with management responsibilities.

1.2 Given the notion that better understanding of schools as organizations will improve their management, the questions arise of where and how to get the requisite knowledge. It used to be thought that such knowledge came only from experience, but over the last twenty years or so there has been a movement in education to follow industry and public administration in treating organizational management as a teachable subject. Accordingly, intending teachers of management in education have set out to look for received wisdom on organizations generally and educational organizations in particular. Now there is a considerable history of theoretical and practical interest in organizations – especially business firms. The written result is best known as 'organization theory' – though it has been variously and confusingly labelled 'administration theory', 'theory of management', 'sociology of organizations', and so on, depending on the semantic and academic affiliations of the authors. The seekers after received wisdom have been disappointed to find that there are serious difficulties with organization theory itself, and that more difficulties appear when attempts are made to employ it in illuminating management in education.

1.3 The difficulties include the unstructured state of organization theory, the multiplicity of theoretical and methodological approaches, the lack of empirical research in schools, the special characteristics of schools as organizations and of the management role in education. These are the topics of section 2 of this unit. It is perhaps unusual in a teaching text to stress problems initially and at length. The reason is that considering these issues helps to establish a (rough) critical framework. This framework is needed *before* examining theoretical approaches to organizations. Since our aim is to arrive at some form of synthesis of knowledge from competing approaches, the most economical way of assembling such a synthesis is to set up criteria for selection or inclusion before interviewing the candidates, i.e. the various theories of organization.

1.4 Section 3 of the unit then reviews some major lines of organization theory. Obviously the account is selective, but this is inevitable within the limited space available. Examples are usually drawn from the secondary school or university. You may find it useful to refer back to the case-study of Unit 2, in which some of the issues are considered at a less theoretical level.

1.5 Our argument has the following sequence:

(a) It is generally assumed that knowledge of schools as organizations will help managers in education.

(b) Unfortunately, organization theory has its own problems and there is no easy way to apply the available generalizations.

(c) A possible approach, however, is to try to form a synthesis from the various organizational perspectives, taking into account the special features of schools as organizations and the role of educational management.

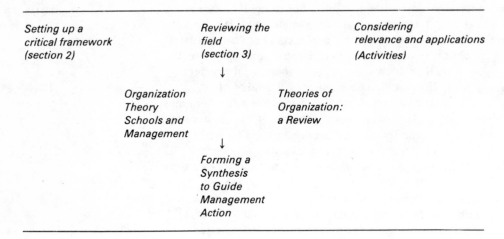

Figure 1   Management Action

1.6 You will find that despite the general-sounding title the unit does not deal with topics of organizational *behaviour*. Such topics as leadership, decision-making and the concept of role are treated elsewhere in the course.

The unit adopts a *management* perspective on schools as organizations. Although there are some sociological readings linked with the unit, management concerns are to the fore. This is reflected in the style of discussions, selection of theories for review, choice of references, and so on.

'Organization' cannot be examined entirely separately from 'management'. Organizations are the environment of management; organizing is a management activity. Hence there is bound to be some overlap with other units. Section 3, for example, overlaps with some parts of Unit 1.

1.7 Effective working of the unit depends upon having a clear picture of its structure and teaching approach. The unit is written as a conscious attempt to overcome a problem which faces many teachers outside the 'hard' sciences – the problem of what one might call 'synchronous theoretical multiplicity'. We find in studying organizations many writers and schools of thought, none exactly right or wrong in empirically testable ways, but all different. If one were writing a text on personality theory in psychology essentially the same difficulties would arise. A radical solution would be for the teacher to analyse the knowledge structure of the subject. Teaching would then be a matter of equipping the student with certain analytic skills and presenting the subject in, say, modes of common ground and theoretical differences as revealed by the second-order study. To carry out this kind of exercise for organization theory would be an enormous research undertaking which nobody has so far attempted. A much more limited attack on the problem is used in the unit, as follows.

1.8 In learning terms, working through the unit you should:

(a) Acquire some basic concepts and impressions of the subject (see paragraph 2.3 on definitions of 'organization' and the readings for section 2, for example).

(b) Develop your own perceptions and experience ('critical framework') of the objects of study, i.e. schools as organizations (see 2.9–2.14), using four variables in characterizing schools as organizations.

(c) Review critically some main approaches to organizational management (section 3), in the light of (a) and (b) above.

Depending on your interpretations and whatever you accept and reject in (c) you should then have some form of 'practical synthesis'. This may indeed contain incompatibilities and will be no 'distillation of truth'. But it will at least be grounded in *your* perceptions and experience. Obviously this synthesizing is not a once-and-for-all process, but a continuing activity for managers who are able to reflect on their work. The unit is, if you like, an *initiation* to the process.

It is, moreover, essentially open-ended and non-prescriptive. (The author's prejudices and attitudes pervade the unit, but you will find plenty of alternatives and correctives in the readings.) Because of this open-ended character some of the conventional features of OU texts have been omitted. It would have been easy but inappropriate to spatter the text with self-assessment questions. Likewise there is no feedback to Activities (save in the case of Activity 1, which is to do with concept acquisition). You may, therefore, find the unit more difficult to cope with than other more conventional units. But if you bear in mind the intentions and functions of the sections, as described here, you should find your task is made easier and, it is hoped, more rewarding.

2.1   Introductory texts on organization theory often begin by stating:

(a)   How important organizations are in our society and thus how important it is for us to understand them.

(b)   How to define 'organization' – what organizations are.
See for example Hicks (set book) Chapters 1 and 2.

Let us follow this precedent.

2.2   The importance of organizations can be readily accepted. Etzioni is highly quotable:

> Our society is an organizational society. We are born in organizations, educated by organizations, and most of us spend much of our lives working for organizations. We spend much of our leisure time paying, playing and praying in organizations. Most of us will die in an organization, and when the time comes for burial, the largest organization of all – the state – must grant official permission.[2]

Organizations, then, are worthy of study though, naturally, actual motives for studying them vary – ranging from the ambition of producing a comprehensive, explanatory theory to the instrumental desire to pass an examination. Study perspectives also vary. Organizations are of interest to psychologists, sociologists, anthropologists and political scientists. The management motive and perspective is essentially pragmatic. Managers act and take decisions within organizations. If their decisions are informed by an understanding of how organizations function they are, it is hoped, the better for it. A head teacher who has the job of building or maintaining the organization of a school will, so our hypothesis runs, achieve better results if he knows something about organizations and how people behave in them than if he proceeds on the usual mix of folk-lore and common-sense. (If this hypothesis is extended to equate knowing about organizations with knowing organization *theory*, it will not be allowed to stand uncriticized, as you will see when we come to consider the Greenfield article in *Reader 1*.) Hicks states that while his reader may well have been unaware of the pervasive influence of organizations on his life it has been there none the less. 'You in turn', he remarks, 'can influence them, if you understand how they work. Instead of being a helpless pawn, you can help to determine how organizations can co-operate to make the best contributions to you and society.'[3] 'Helpless pawn' is perhaps an exaggeration, but the over-all message is one you will find echoed by many writers on management.

2.3   The definition of 'organization' takes us into deeper water. This is so despite the fact that 'organization' is a term in common use and has already been used several times in this unit without serious risk of misunderstanding. It is this very fact – that 'organization' is an ordinary-language concept – which tends to create definitional problems when social scientists borrow and redefine it for special purposes. The ordinary-language definition of 'organization' can be found in any dictionary. The Concise Oxford Dictionary connects 'organization' with the ideas of 'orderly structure', 'working order', 'arrangements' and 'co-operation'. In some senses, parts of the physical work are 'organizations', irrespective of whether people are involved in them or not. Cartwright is referring to these highly general senses when he writes of an organization as 'an arrangement of interdependent parts each having a special function with regard to the whole'.[4] A pair of scissors or a tree would presumably qualify as this kind of 'organization'. The main-line meaning is bound up with what Cartwright refers to as the 'social entity' – i.e. groups of people engaged in activities. Now although the whole of social life is 'organized' in that patterns and relationships between individuals can be discerned, *organization theory,* as a rule, is concerned only with certain types of organized social life. These are termed 'formal' or 'complex' organizations which typically are said to have the features of being deliberately established for certain purposes, possessing rules, status and authority structures, clearly marked lines of communication, and persistence over time. A school is thus a formal organization, but a friendship group is probably not. For organization theory, 'organization' = 'formal organization', and it is with the definition of this type of social entity that we are now concerned.[5]

There are three features of definitions of the (formal) 'organization' which should be noted:

(a) 'Organization' has occasionally been defined so widely as to be almost meaningless. Hicks (1972) for example, says, 'An organization is a structured process in which people interact for objectives'. He goes on to include cases of people meeting accidentally for a few seconds in the street as 'bona fide organizations'.[6] Hicks admits that this is 'unexpected', but you may ask yourself how useful a definition is which produces such unexpected results. His definition is so broad as to include almost all possible social groups and encounters – a football crowd, an amorous meeting, buying a bus ticket. It seems odd to refer to these as 'organizations', and the fact that they may all be worthy of study by, say, social psychologists, is no good reason to give them all the same label – especially a label drawn from ordinary usage with a normally restricted meaning.

(b) It is possible to fall into the error of looking for some special single property supposedly common to all the organizations in which theorists have traditionally been interested. The pursuing of 'goals' is a tempting choice. Given that we are going to study schools, business firms, armies, churches and hospitals, we may be inclined to say that because all these 'formal' or 'complex' organizations have organizational goals – for example educating children, making a profit, defending the country – it is the pursuing of such goals that differentiates such organizations from the more 'social' friendship group, family or community. This restrictive type of definition is likely to lead to fruitless argument about what constitutes an organizational goal, how it may be identified and how it relates to the goals of individuals within formal organizations. This may be at the expense of other possibly more significant organizational properties. Silverman discusses the general problems which arise from definitions of organizations in terms of goals. You should read his discussion if you wish to pursue this issue.[7]

Here we need only note that to search for the single defining property of a concept is a well-known possible route to confusion. Wittgenstein provides a piece of philosophical therapy:

> Consider for example the proceedings that we call 'games'. I mean board-games, card-games, ball-games, Olympic games and so on. What is common to them all? – Don't say: 'There *must* be something common, or they would not be called "games" ' – but *look and see* whether there is anything common to all. – For if you look at them you will not see something that is common to *all*, but similarities, relationships, and a whole series of them at that.[8]

The network of similarities between games can be regarded as 'family resemblances'. Our suggestion is that different kinds of organization too – schools, business firms and the rest – form a 'family' with various overlapping and criss-crossing features. To accept this suggestion is to see the futility of searching for the common, single 'defining property'.

(c)   Organization theorists tend to be programmatic in defining the objects of their study. You may find in the literature definitions of an organization as 'a set of social meanings' or as 'an input–output system' or 'a system of co-operative human activities'. These are not necessarily conflicting definitions. They are more like announcements of the author's intentions to look at organizations in a particular way. And there is no shortage of ways to choose. Just as a school can legimately be conceived of as a building, a learning environment or an expenditure centre, so organizations, as we shall see, can be conceived of in many different ways. Clark Kerr, Chancellor of the University of California at Berkeley, was said to have conceived of the university more as a system of parking lots than a community of scholars.[9] These are revealing than contradictory 'definitions' of a university.

So it is with many definitions of 'organization'. They simply reveal which of a number of alternative (legitimate) organizations the author has in mind. Thus, while it is true that 'the term "organization" belongs to the category of expressions about which there is maintained an air of informed vagueness, certain special conventions exist that focus its use, with qualifications, on a delimited set of phenomena'.[10] In studying organization theory you should be aware of these conventions and qualifications. You should also be sensitive to over-general, restrictive and programmatic definitions.

The extract from Etzioni (1964) reprinted below gives a short account of his own definition of organizations. As you see, he limits the field of usage and lists a number of characteristics instead of insisting on a single defining property. He also mentions such possible synonyms as 'bureaucracy' and 'institution'. His definition is programmatic – by exclusion, as it were – but not exceptionally narrow. Etzioni is setting the scene for an approach to organizations based, as he says later, on a synthesis of the formal scientific management and the informal human-relations approaches. He is by virtue of his definition no systems man or phenomenologist.

Organizations Defined

Organizations are social units (or human groupings) deliberately constructed and reconstructed to seek specific goals. Corporations, armies, schools, hospitals, churches, and prisons are included; tribes, classes, ethnic groups, friendship groups, and families are excluded. Organizations are characterized by: (1) divisions of labor, power, and communication responsibilities, divisions which are not random or traditionally patterned, but deliberately planned to enhance the realization of specific goals; (2) the presence of one or more power centers which control the concerted efforts of the organization and direct them toward its goals; these power centers also must review continuously the organization's performance and re-pattern its structure, where necessary, to increase its efficiency; (3) substitution of personnel, i.e., unsatisfactory persons can be removed and others assigned their tasks. The organization can also recombine its personnel through transfer and promotion.

Other social units are marked by some degree of conscious planning (e.g., the family budget), by the existence of power centers (e.g., tribal chiefs), and by replaceable membership (e.g., through divorce), but the extent to which these other social units are consciously planned, deliberately structured and restructured, with a membership which is routinely changed, is much less than in the case of those social units we are calling *organizations*. Hence organizations are much more in control of their nature and destiny than any other social grouping.

There are many synonyms for the term, *organization*. One, *bureaucracy*, has two disadvantages. First, *bureaucracy* often carries a negative connotation for the layman, while *organization* is a neutral term. Second, *bureaucracy* implies for those familiar with Weber's work . . . that the unit is organized according to the principles he specified. But many organizations, including many modern ones, are not bureaucratic in this technical sense.

Hospitals, for instance, do not have one center of decision-making, whereas bureaucracies do, by definition. *Formal organization* refers to one set of characteristics of organizations . . . this term does not refer to an organization as an entity, but only to a part of it. *Institution* is sometimes used to refer to certain types of organizations, either quite respectable ones as in 'GM is an institution,' or quite unrespectable ones, as in 'He is in an institution.' Sometimes institution refers to a quite different phenomenon – namely, to a normative principle that culturally defines behavior such as marriage or property. Because of these two conflicting usages, this term has probably caused more confusion than *formal organization* and *bureaucracy* together. All three might well be avoided in favor of the simple term, *organization*.

Since many social groupings have some degree of patterning and some control structure – e.g., in contrast to a mob – *social organization* has been used to characterize these phenomena. But in recent years *social structure* has been increasingly employed to describe these characteristics of social units. Thus we can safely reserve the term *organizations* to refer to planned units, deliberately structured for the purpose of attaining specific goals, and do without social organizations, altogether.[11]

Activity 1

Read Chapters 1 and 2 of Hicks (set book). You may find it useful to look first at the summaries on pp. 16–17 and 34–35 of the book. Chapter 1 is about the reasons why organizations exist and the ways in which organizations can be classified. Chapter 2 describes the interaction of individuals in organizations. Wherever possible, try to relate the concepts introduced and the illustrations given by Hicks to the school. You may consider using the Sidney Stringer material from the case study in Unit 2 as a point of reference.

The purpose of this activity is to broaden your view of organizations and to introduce some basic concepts of organization theory. In the text we have mentioned only the reasons for studying organizations and how they may be defined. The additional groundwork provided by this reading is essential to a full appreciation of later sections of the unit.

Then answer the following:

(a) On pp. 14–15 Hicks introduces the idea of organizations on a continuum between 'formal' and 'informal' ideal types. In the light of this, do you think it was unfair to criticize his definition (on p. 23) of an organization as being so wide as 'to be almost meaningless'? Might not his examples of accidental meetings, and so on, simply find their place at the extreme informal end of the continuum?

(b) (See Hicks p. 17, Q. 1.) Explain why you are a member of the Open University, pointing out the things you give up for membership and the benefits you expect to receive.

(c) Give examples of Hicks's four levels of interaction, with reference to the school as an organization (Hicks, pp. 26–8).

(d) (See Hicks, p. 35, Q. 8.) For a teacher in a school give (possible) examples of
(i) personal objectives,
(ii) his–her concept of the organization's objectives.

(e) What, according to Hicks, would be the over-all objectives of the school as an organization?

You should spend about one hour on this Activity.

(a) The criticism is fair despite the introduction of the continuum idea. If one allows accidental meetings as (very) informal organizations one might as well allow a pile of bricks to qualify as a (very) rudimentary building.

(b) You give up fees, time and a range of other possibilities to which you might give your resources and attention. Your answer to the benefits question depends on your needs and your honesty in recognizing them.

(c) Individuals interact –
Example: Student–Teacher.
Individuals and the organization interact –
Example: Individual reaction to school rules.
Organizations and other organizations interact –
Example: School–Local Education Authority.
Organizations and their total environment interact –
Example: School goes comprehensive in response to national legislation–policy.

(d) Examples:
(i)   Money, personal–professional satisfaction.
(ii) Transmitting a cultural heritage, combating illiteracy.

(e) The overall objectives of the school as an organization, according to Hicks, would be the total of individual concepts of those objectives given on pp. 28–31. He suggests that to speak of an organization as an entity with its own objectives is a 'verbal short cut'.

Figure 2–3 on p. 31 of Hicks makes the point again. There is an obvious difficulty with this view: i.e., whose concepts of the school's objectives are to be included? Staff, students, parents, employers, administrators – how long is the list to be?

2.4 Having taken the conventional first steps of considering the importance and definition of organizations, we are now set to examine organization theory proper. The immediate problem to confront us is that there is no single entity which answers to the name 'organization theory'. What we find is a bewildering variety of different theories, methodologies, conceptual schemes and ideologies.

Scott said over ten years ago 'there does not yet exist a single, widely accepted theory of organizations'.[12] The same statement would find a consensus of opinion today. In Unit 1 Colin Morgan suggested that the study of management could be regarded as a 'lake' formed by the confluence of different rivers of knowledge. This may be an appropriate metaphor to depict the merging of techniques and approaches in management practice. But if we apply that metaphor to organization theory then the trouble is that the 'rivers' do not seem to flow into the same 'lake'. Indeed one writer, facetiously but aptly, has gone so far as to compare organization theorists with children in a sandpit indulging in what Piaget called a 'collective monologue'.[13]

2.5   The sheer diversity of organization theory may be illustrated by noting some of the methods which it has been necessary to adopt for surveying the field. Approaches to organizations can be surveyed as 'schools of thought'.

Thus management textbooks commonly select (as in section 3 of this unit)
Classical Theory
Bureaucracy
Human Relations
Systems Approaches
as four broad categories, each of which can be subdivided. Newer 'schools' include the 'social action' and 'phenomenological' perspectives, among others.

Alternatively, a typology of approaches may be used. Weeks, for example, uses a series of dichotomies (see also Hoyle in his article in *Reader 1*), as shown in the following table.

Table 1 Distinctions between approaches to organizations

Distinctions	Deductive, determinist approach	Inductive, voluntaristic approach
Theoretical	System Universalist Formal Unitary Structure	Action* Particularist Informal Pluralist Process
Methodological	Functionalist Comparative Analysis	Historical Case Study
Substantive	Mechanistic High specificity of role prescription	Organismic Low specificity of role prescription

From Weeks, D. R. (1973) 'Organization theory – some themes and distinctions', in Salaman, G. and Thompson, K., (see note 10), p. 390.

Another possibility is to distinguish between levels of analysis:

Role analysis – concentrating on the individual role in relation to the function of the organization.

Structural analysis – dealing with organizational groups and the structural features of organizations.

Organizational analysis – studying the characteristics of organizations themselves and their relations.[14]

Or, again, organization studies may be viewed in terms of purposes. These may be either:

Descriptive – aiming to explain the processes of organizations, or

Prescriptive (normative) – aiming to state what the processes *should be* for the sake of organization efficiency.[15]

Not all the above terms, especially those in Weeks's typology, will be familiar. Some will be explained later in the course. The intention here is merely to convey the diversity of approaches.

2.6 Now it might be that the diverse character of organization theory is a temporary matter, the sort of state any new field of study might be in before becoming an integrated discipline. After all, the words 'not yet' were used by Scott in his statement quoted above. Or if the emergence of an integrated discipline is too much to hope for with organization theory generally, can we not hope at least for some unity of approach to schools as organizations? Hoyle, writing from a sociological rather than a management viewpoint, considers the variety of approaches to the organizational analysis of schools, and concludes:

> ... there has ... been a degree of optimism about a possible convergence which would provide a distinctive theoretical perspective and body of research to illustrate the functioning of schools and to resolve practical problems arising from their day-to-day operations. These expectations have been fulfilled to a lesser degree than was anticipated in the early 1960s. Some convergence has taken place, but there remain considerable differences in approach, and it may well be that a full understanding of schools will be best derived from different sorts of study.[16]

*Weeks states that 'this first distinction [i.e. between system and action approaches] sets the tone for all the others in that they are all in some way variations on this main theme' (p.379).

While it is not obvious what would count as 'a full understanding of schools', we can concur with Hoyle that the convergence of approaches has been limited, and the outlook for more convergence is not encouraging. The problem is likely to remain.

2.7 One solution to the problem of diversity would be to stake everything on one particular approach. For example as Pugh says:

> Organization theory is the body of thinking and writing which addresses itself to the problem of how to organize . . .
> More specifically organization theory can be defined as the study of the structure, functioning and performance of organizations and the behaviour of groups and individuals within them.[17]
>
> All organizations have to be managed . . .[18]

These definitions indicate the scenario to come. We would take the prescriptive – 'how to organize' – rather than the descriptive line. We would study 'structure' and 'performance' of schools rather than, say, 'social meanings'. The guiding premiss would be that all this was grist to the 'management' mill. But to take a single approach, however consistent, and to ignore the major alternatives would be biased and restrictive from a teaching angle. Another solution would be to take, like Hicks (in the Preface to the set book, p. xxvi), an 'uncomplicated, broad, introductory systems view of the field of organizations', aiming to present 'an integrated study' while omitting the 'merits and disadvantages' of comparative theories along with their historical aspects. But given the complex and conflicting nature of organization theory, it is impossible to take an 'uncomplicated' view in the interests of 'integrated study' without accepting a policy of systematic distortion. It is difficult also to avoid some discussion of 'merits and disadvantages' in an educational *management* course. And surely there is some connection between organization theory and social history. Both solutions have the attractions of simplicity. Either would make this unit easier to write and to study. Both, unfortunately, would also be thoroughly misleading. One may accept with the best will in the world Dewey's celebrated dictum that theory is in the end the most practical of all things. The question remains: Which theory? The approach of this unit will be that since an integrated organization theory does not exist, a possible way forward is to try to form a synthesis from the available perspectives. If the synthesis is to be of practical value then it has to be based on insights and criteria derived from the actual organizations and activities which interest us – i.e. schools and their management. Our perceptions of schools and the management role in them will determine the critical framework within which a synthesis may be established.

2.8 Some of the distinctive features of educational organizations were discussed in the final sections of Unit 1. Let us now return to these themes and attempt to characterize schools as organizations. Three complications arise with any such effort.

First, there are enormous variations between educational institutions along several dimensions. Even if we avoid the Kindergarten–Cambridge gross variation by restricting ourselves to, say, secondary schools, variations of many kinds remain. Size, location, type – for example public, grammar, comprehensive – are just a few of the possibilities.

Second, 'There is a large gap between the paucity of our empirical knowledge of educational organizations (considering the British and US output together) and our willingness to make assumptions about the similarities and shared features of schools and colleges.'[19] In other words we don't know much and we must not jump to conclusions. So caution is called for, plus an honest admission that there is bound to be a certain arbitrariness about our chosen categories and concepts.

Third,

> Perhaps all educational institutions display certain 'essential features', all, for instance, having basic 'fundamental prerequisites', 'boundary problems', or 'staff and student echelons'; perhaps they all can usefully be thought of as

contributing towards the system's 'functions' of culture transmission, selection, allocation, and so on. The point is that this whole apparatus of terms used to display relationship, fit, and order obscures certain sorts of issues by sharpening our awareness of others. What comes to sensitize stays to suppress.[20]

These remarks are directed against the systems approach to the complexity of educational institutions. We must not allow the seductive 'neatness and simplicity' of models to obscure reality. The points made in the last two sentences of the quotation, however, are well taken.

2.9   Having noted the dangers, let us press on, if not regardless at least undaunted. The following discussion of the distinctive features of schools as organizations will be based on four variables which seem especially relevant.

Goals – What are the aims and
    objectives?

Technology – How are the objectives
    to be attained? What tasks and
    methods are involved?

Participation – Who participates in membership
    and decisions?

Values – What values do the
    organization–individuals serve?

18

We shall draw on the views of four writers: Davies (1973), March (1974), Willower (1973) and Scheffler (1973). Those of you who are sensitive to the culture base of pronouncements on education may note that the first of the above writers is from the United Kingdom and the remainder from North America.

The goals of educational organizations are problematic

2.10   March, who regards schools as 'organized anarchies' sums it up thus:

> It is difficult to specify a consistent set of goals. Instead goals seem to shift over time; they seem to vary from one part of the organization to another; they seem to be stated in terms that are hard to translate into action. There is conflict over goals, and the conflict is not resolved easily. Although it is sometimes possible to impute goals to the organization by observing behaviour, such imputations appear often to be unstable or to define goals that are not acceptable to all participants in the organization. The decision process seems to reflect more a series of actions by which goals are discovered than a process by which they are acted upon. Speeches on goals express platitudes that are not useful administratively.[21]

This aspect of schools creates immediate worries for theorists who rate 'goals' high in the scheme of things. One problem, of course, is 'Whose goals?' Although, for example, staff and students have different status, the goals of both affect the structure and functioning of the school. The goals of these two groups may be conflicting. Two ways out suggest themselves. First, the problem can be reduced by regarding students not as members but as the materials processed by the organization. The 'materials', unfortunately, have the human properties of being able to influence and disagree. Another possibility is to refer to the original purposes for which the organization was created – the 'charter'. But it is at least conceivable that there is no longer any member of the organization who would subscribe to these. The result is implausibility. Neither solution is satisfactory. (Unit 7, *The Role of Objectives*, discusses objectives in education in more detail.)

No theory of organization which requires the rational pursuit of clear and agreed organizational goals will fit schools.

The technology of schooling is unclear

2.11   March expresses the problem thus:

> Although we know how to create an educational institution, to staff it, and to specify an educational program for it, we do not know much about the process by which it works. It does work, at least in some senses. Students seem to change. Moreover, we can duplicate our results. If we recreate the procedures in a new school, they will often have approximately the same outcomes. But we have remarkably little capability for designing change in the system. We do not, in general, know what will happen if we make changes; we do not, in general, know how to adapt the standard system to non-standard students or situations. New occasions require a new set of trial-and-error procedures, either in the school or in an experimental laboratory.[22]

This is not the place to debate whether the above propositions are entirely true, what qualifications need to be entered, what 'educational technology' might be or might contribute, and so on. We shall take it that by and large the tasks which teachers perform and the methods they use are not well understood compared with the tasks and methods of engineers. What then are the consequences? One result is that the school as an organization cannot easily fit the bureaucratic or formal models. Lines of authority, division of labour, rules and procedures are all more difficult to specify in an organization lacking a clear technology. There is more room for craft, experience, 'art' and the myths and recipes of the practitioner – 'When you take on a new class you have to show them you're the boss, otherwise . . .' New teachers do not so much learn how to teach as become socialized to the norms of their colleagues. As Willower puts it, ' . . . coping takes precedence over planning. The school is not organized in a manner that facilitates the use of explanatory systems to confront problems. Rather its normative and formal structures are devoted in large part to adaptations that function to reduce the demands upon the organization to manageable proportions.'[23] Another result is to be found in the stabilizing operations which go on in the school. Because the technology of the school, i.e. the nature of the tasks performed, does not impose its own routines, it is necessary for routines to be created. An example is the near-standard lesson period of approximately forty minutes found in schools. This has little justification in theory or research – but it does tend to introduce stability. All organizations maintain such structures for the sake of stability and to reduce uncertainty and risk. It would seem likely that the more uncertainty and risk there are, the more routinization and other stabilizing structures will be needed. Unclear technology means high uncertainty and risk. Those of you who are teachers or have good memories may care to compile a list of school routines and rituals; and then consider how these relate or fail to relate to the teaching task.

No theory of organization will fit schools unless it is able to take account of the results of unclear technology in organizations.

Participation in schools as organizations is fluid

2.12   As March puts it:

> Participants come and go. Students, teachers, and administrators move in and out. There is even more turnover in other participants or potential participants. Parents, individually and collectively, are erratic in their involvement; community leaders sometimes ignore the schools, sometimes devote considerable time to them; government agencies are active, then passive. All the potential actors in the organizations have other concerns that compete with the school for their attention. Thus, whether they participate in the school depends as much on the changing characteristics of their alternatives as it does on the characteristics of the educational organization involved.[24]

There are two points here. The first is that participation in schools is 'fluid' in the sense that it is unpredictable and varies over time. The second is that the fluidity exists largely because of the way in which schools as organizations are 'open' to the environment. The boundaries are permeable and the 'causal texture' – to use Emery and Trist's phrase – of the environment is problematic.[25] A given school exists as a unit in a wider social and administrative setting. Its basic existence is shaped by government, tradition and the legal system. The school is also a 'service organization', which is there to serve the interests of a primary clientele of students.[26] But what those interests are and how they may best be served is not pre-determined. Hence the school is open to a wide range of demands and influences which determine what actually goes on within the permitted framework. Schools receive demands from internal participants – staff and students. They also receive demands from outside – employers, parents, local and national political groups, professional advisers, purveyors of educational innovations, textbook authors, examining boards, publishers and local-authority administrators, to name but some of the possible participants. As a result, to quote Davies, 'we would expect to find either that schools are highly successful at reconciling a number of widely differing demands or that they tend to develop devices for insulation against some of the pressures facing them'.[27]

At Sidney Stringer School, studied in Unit 2, there was evidence of an attempt to systematize and clarify the interrelationships between the various groups of participants both within and outside the school who had some claim to influence the running of it. The material suggests that consensus on who should have influence, and where, is difficult to achieve; also that formal attempts to redistribute the balance of influence from the top do not necessarily overcome traditional patterns based on existing power resources.

No theory of organization will fit schools unless it is able to provide for the special organizational problems posed by fluid participation, resolution of conflict, and boundary maintenance.

As educational agencies schools are necessarily involved with the moral, social and intellectual values which education entails.

2.13 Willower states the issues thus:

> In the school setting, values and ideals are often proclaimed but the relation to goal achievement of such statements, largely nonoperational in nature, remains cloaked in blessed obscurity. The expression of educational ideals may be made for internal or for external consumption. Declarations of educational philosophy ordinarily found in curricular guides but having little impact on the curriculum are examples of the former. The external orientation is illustrated in statements concerning school programs disseminated through the public media. Such statements recount successes and invoke values thought to be widely held; they are rarely devoted to failure or controversy. These exercises in public relations are organizational manifestations of 'on stage behavior' and impression management. They enhance organizational stability by countering anticipated or real environmental forces which could disturb the adjustment of the system. While the enunciation of educational ideals is functional for the school in this sense, whether it has salutary effects for students is unclear. Here, the difficulty of assessing the school's outputs adds confusion to an already-blurred picture. If ideals are not achieved or even approximated no one may be the wiser. Similarly, if they are attained, it may remain a well-kept secret. After all, 'good teaching throws a short shadow.'
>
> However, some sets of values are likely to gain both professed and actual adherence from schools and educators: values reflected in societal and community norms. In fact, it is not unusual to find an exaggerated conformity to such standards. In any case, especially since the young are entrusted to its stewardship, the school must appear to be in step with dominant, but often unexamined, community values; while in the realm of educational ideals, its deeds are less certain than its words.[28]

We can accept that value statements are non-operational in that prescriptions for specific action are difficult or impossible to derive from them. Willower goes on to suggest that such value declarations in education are required for stability and as a means of impression management. In fact the issue is a deeper one. 'Education' is a value-laden concept, as philosophers of education tirelessly remind their students. To claim that an activity is 'educational' is, they assert, to invoke three criteria:

(a) That the activity is valuable in itself;

(b) That the activity is associated with other activities, so that there is a wide cognitive perspective, i.e. it is seen to relate to other ways of understanding and experiencing;

(c) That those who are engaged in the activity come to care for it, come to think that it is worth doing.[29]

The nature of the logical connection between 'education' and 'values' is not simple, but it seems reasonable to accept that one or more of the above criteria does apply when distinguishing education from other sorts of activities. And certainly it is logically odd to assert that an activity is both 'educational' and 'valueless' or 'not worth-while'. Transferring to the realm of practical decisions, it follows that 'there is no decision about education which is "value-free" or "neutral" '.[30]

It is with some trepidation that a philosophical point is introduced in a text dealing with management in education. But it is salutary to do so, because of the constant tension in education between the 'instrumental' versus the 'expressive', or 'transmission' versus the 'expression' models (see Unit 1, paragraphs 5.4 and 5.5). Management in education treads an uneasy path between the instrumental drive for efficiency and the expressive value-bound nature of the educational process. As Harris puts it in the concluding sentence of his article in *Reader 2,* (Reading 1.1) 'Management in education is about what education *ought* to achieve as well as about *how* to achieve it'. The student of E321 will do well to cultivate a philosophically keen sense for recognition of 'ought' and 'how' statements in his reading. Values, tasks and organization in schools are intrinsically connected. Consider the following views of Scheffler:

> The transmission model in education, coupled with the drive for increased efficiency, tends to foster the view of the teacher as a minor technician within an industrial process. The over-all goals are set in advance in terms of national needs, the curricular materials prepackaged by the disciplinary experts, the methods developed by educational engineers – and the teacher's job is just to supervise the last operational stage, the methodical insertion of ordered facts into the student's mind. Teacher competence is to be judged (at most) in terms of academic mastery and pedagogical dexterity, and teacher education becomes identified with training in the subject, coupled with training in the approved methods of teaching.

> In my view, this picture is radically wrong. The teacher in a free society is not just a technician. He ought to have a voice in shaping the purposes of the whole educational enterprise. In any event, he influences students not just by what he *does* but by what he *is*, not just by the facts he provides but by the *questions* he provokes. He needs a basic flexibility of mind, a capacity to step outside his subject and consider it from without together with his student, a fundamental respect for the student's mind, and a willingness to encourage new ideas, doubts, questions and puzzlements. If he is to fulfill his function properly, he must be viewed not just as a technician but as a free mind alive to radical questions concerning the foundations of his subject, its relations to other areas, and its applications in society. He must be trained not just as an applied specialist but as a free and critical intellect.[31]

Note that the entire second paragraph is a series of explicit and implicit value statements. Such statements cannot be justified by appeals to facts. Scheffler is expounding his beliefs about education and encouraging us to share them. There is no doubt that most teachers are closer in self-image to Scheffler's second model –

22

'the free and critical intellect' – than to his first – 'the minor technician within an industrial process' – though the cynic might hint at a possible gap between aspiration and reality. What matters for our purpose is to observe that not only do teachers and learners *necessarily* have values (which may, of course, differ widely) to do with students, knowledge, freedom, etc., but that these tend to be seen in opposition to the instrumental world of efficiency. Such values must be to some extent determinants of educational organizations.

No theory of organization which does not allow for the relevance of values, other than the instrumental variety, will fit schools.

2.14   The time has come for a little more of the 'caution' and 'honest admission' mentioned above. Our four variables – goals, technology, participation and values – are not the only possible choices. 'Power', 'authority', or 'culture' could have been selected.

We have committed assorted sins of provocation, omission and simplification. Discussion of each variable has ended with a negative statement about the type of organization theorizing which will *not* fit schools. Repentance is inappropriate so long as we have been successful in the teaching objective of stimulating you to think about the distinctive organizational features of schools.

What is important now is that you should develop your own perception of the school as an organization. The four-variable framework is a device for you to use in this process. Activity 2 gives you the chance to inject your own thoughts and to put a positive cast on specifying the sort of synthesis from organization theory which may in your opinion assist in school management.

Activity 2

Re-read paragraphs 2.10 to 2.13, marking in the text points where you would disagree with the statements made or where you have comments of your own to make.

Then:

(a)   Without referring again to the text make notes on each variable – goals, technology, participation and values. Ask yourself the question 'What is distinctive about the school as an organization?' with regard to each variable. Wherever possible use your own perceptions and experience of schools.

(b)   Rewrite the four negative statements at the end of paragraphs 2.10–2.13 to form a positive prescription with which you would agree. 'A synthesis of organization theory to fit schools will need to . . .'

This activity will enable you to develop your own thinking about schools as organizations. If you are involved with schools in your work it will also enable you to relate the generalities of the text to real situations. You may find it useful to refer to your work on the 'congruence' question in Unit 1 and to the case-study material in Unit 2.

You should allow one hour for this Activity.

2.15   Despair may be setting in at this image of the school as an institutional morass of diffuse goals, values, etc. But one can take heart from March's view that although schools are 'organized anarchies' these are not unusual organizations. 'Indeed', he writes, 'they are quite common. Decision situations involving problematic goals, unclear technology and fluid participation are familiar to all types of organizations. They do, however, pose some problems for administrators, and particularly for our standard theories of administrative action.'[32]

We need to ask, then, *What sort of organizational problems (decision situations) do school administrators–managers face?* Another question is suggested by Davies. After acknowledging the 'conceptual, theoretical, empirical and even ideological obstacles to organizational studies in education', he goes on to encourage us by asserting that these obstacles are 'probably no greater than those existing in any other area . . . ' But 'what is certainly the case is that there can be no substitute in the study of educational organizations for empirical work in schools, colleges and educational administrative bodies themselves'.[33] Our question is, for schools, *What relevant empirical research has been carried out*? We shall now look briefly at these two questions.

Margaret Maden, Head of Islington Green Comprehensive School

Problems of organizational management in schools

2.16 For simplicity let us concentrate on the management role of the head. This is often described in highly general terms. One head of a comprehensive school in Gloucestershire is quoted as saying:

> Externally the Head has to convey the ethos and interpret the aims of the school to the community. Internally he has to frame policy and plan the delegation of responsibility to ensure maximum efficiency, in putting theory into practice: he must attempt to create an atmosphere in which staff can work in harmony and pupils develop in security, maintaining the balance between stability and innovation.[34]

Note the words 'efficiency', 'harmony', 'security' and 'balance'. These are the (vague) states at which he aims. Note also 'interpret', 'frame', 'plan', 'create', 'maintain'. These are the (vague) activities in which he engages. Such states and activities are far removed from operations and behaviour. The description as a whole is so general that with a few appropriate verbal substitutions it could stand as an account of the function of the Chairman of British Rail, or of an Archbishop.

We might well ask: what counts as 'efficiency', 'harmony', and so on in schools? How would the head recognize, measure and compare these states? And what do 'interpreting', 'framing', 'ensuring' and the rest consist of in terms of what the head actually does? To apply our hypothesis that organization theory can assist him in dealing with management problems we require an indication of what these problems are. General descriptions of the above kind are no help.

Some information is provided by diary research into the ways in which heads spend their working time. This has been advocated by Taylor.[35] An illustration from another source of the way in which one head spent his time is given in Table 2.

Table 2 How a headmaster spends his time

Description of activity	Time taken estimate	Regular or occasional
Preparation of Prayers and Assembly	15–20 mins.	Regular
Taking School Prayers, announcements, etc.	20 mins.	Regular
Sorting mail, dealing with matters arising, distributing information to staff	30 mins.	Regular
Dictation of letters	30 mins.	Regular
Meeting people:	2 hours +	Regular
(a) *Official* (Clerk of Works, Visiting Inspectors, Elect. Engrs., Architects Dept., Police, etc.)		
(b) *Medical* (doctor, nurse, dentist)		
(c) *Unofficial* (charities, parents, workmen reporting in, etc.)		
(d) *Staff* (teachers bringing requests, suggestions or discussing problems (often personal))		
(e) *Children* (disciplinary, seeking advice, vandalism)		
Investigation:	30 mins.	Occasional
(a) Serious cases of lost or stolen property	In some	
(b) Fabric in cases of damage or dealing with workmen or accompanying Clerk of Works	cases considerably longer	
Planning:	Averaging	Occasional
Time-tables, schemes of work in conjunction with staff. Special activities, e.g. prize-giving, sports, eisteddfod, exams, terminals (with rearranged classes)	5 hours per week	
Answering telephone calls and making outgoing calls	30–60 mins.	Regular
School meals – overall supervision	30 mins.	Regular
Completion of forms – ministerial, L.E.A.	30 mins. +	Occasional
Completing school log and records	10 mins.	Regular
Educational bodies requiring statistics	1 hour in a term	Occasional
Cleaning staff: dealing with problems brought by cleaning staff via caretaker, problems of heating, complaints re fuel, etc.	15–30 mins.	Occasional

From Hughes, M. G. (ed.) (1970) *Secondary School Administration*, op. cit., (see note 34), p. 81.

A likely result of this sort of research, according to Taylor, would be to establish that 'the public image of headship gives too much credit for long term planning, and not enough for the difficulties of coping with the administrative and interpersonal minutiae of the daily round'. Parallel findings have been gained from research in business organizations. The Sidney Stringer case study gives an example of a deliberate attempt to redress the balance, freeing more time for long-term planning by a system of delegation and participation in decision-making.

But, for our purposes, diary research takes us too far in the operational direction. At one level we saw the head's job as framing policies and creating atmospheres; now we see the job as answering the telephone and completing forms. A middle ground of description needs to be found if we are to identify the key problems of the manager in education.

One method of proceeding is to attend to the head's role as a decision-maker in the organization. We can then use a classification scheme to isolate the type of decisions that the head makes which give rise to problems. Simon has distinguished two polar types of decisions which he calls 'programmed' and 'non-programmed' respectively. Programmed decisions are routine, with a definite procedure for handling them; they tend to be repetitive and unproblematic. Non-programmed decisions are novel and unstructured; no routines exist for dealing with them and they tend to be elusive, complex and consequential.[36] Obviously there is a continuum here, with, in Simon's words, 'all shades of gray' along it. Also it needs to be said that some decisions, although perfectly capable of being programmed, i.e. dealt with by, say, clerical procedures or statistics, are treated in some organizations as non-programmed. (See also Unit 1, paragraph 3.5).

In a course on management for teachers (including heads, deputy heads and others from primary and further education levels) at Warwick University during 1973–4, I used the Simon programmed–non-programmed dichotomy to assist course members in stating the management problems they faced. This work is described in a forthcoming book.[37] No general conclusions can be reached, but the results which emerged possibly indicate some issues to which management courses in education should pay special attention. The following is a representative sample of those teachers' views on the organizational problems they face in schools.

Geoff Cooksey, Director, Stantonbury Campus, Milton Keynes at a staff discussion.

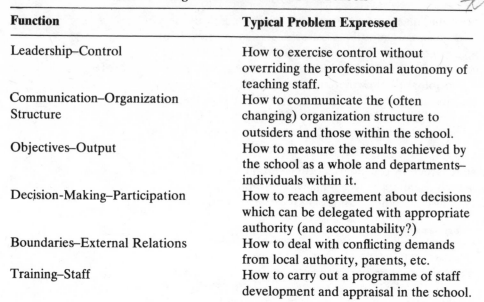

Table 3 Organizational Problems in Schools

Function	Typical Problem Expressed
Leadership–Control	How to exercise control without overriding the professional autonomy of teaching staff.
Communication–Organization Structure	How to communicate the (often changing) organization structure to outsiders and those within the school.
Objectives–Output	How to measure the results achieved by the school as a whole and departments–individuals within it.
Decision-Making–Participation	How to reach agreement about decisions which can be delegated with appropriate authority (and accountability?)
Boundaries–External Relations	How to deal with conflicting demands from local authority, parents, etc.
Training–Staff	How to carry out a programme of staff development and appraisal in the school.

There was a high level of agreement among the fifty or so course members that these problems were among the most pressing. Many others were raised and discussed, but the above six instances will serve here as illustrations.

The problems above are not expressed in over-general or over-specific terms. They are not trival yet it is possible to get to grips with them. It is worth noting, however, that it is hard to find a theoretically neutral way of stating organizational problems. Heads of schools, like managers elsewhere, tend to conceptualize and relate their problems in theoretically loaded terms. Some tend to use expressions such as 'responsibility', 'authority', and 'chain of command'; others talk more of 'relationships', referring to these as 'open', 'distant', 'cohesive', etc. The first set is, of course, the language of classical theory; the latter concepts are those emphasized by human-relations theorists. These two approaches are merely the commonest among the possible alternatives.[38] The result is that the same phenomenon can be described by, say, a traditionalist as a problem of 'insubordination', while a follower of recent organizational fashion might see it as a 'procedural breakdown'. The way in which heads perceive and state their organizational problems often prescribes also the solutions which they will accept. And even if the concepts and assumptions used do not together deserve the name 'theory', they still form what McGregor has called a managerial 'cosmology' within which both problems and solutions exist.[39]

Activity 3

If your interest in this course is a practical one – and management courses in education, as elsewhere, are bound to address themselves primarily to the practitioner – then you may find it useful at this point to consider the sorts of organizational problems which you actually face in your work.

Use the six problems listed above in Table 3 as a starting point. How far do these apply in your case? If you find the problems relevant, what shape do they assume, i.e. what decisions relating to them do you have to take? What problems would you add to or substitute on the list? You may find the programmed–non-programmed dichotomy useful in considering these questions.

The purpose of this activity is to supplement Activity 2 for those of you who have present practical concerns with schools as organizations.

You should allow thirty minutes for this Activity.

2.17 The short answer to the second question in paragraph 2.15 above is that relevant empirical research into schools as organizations is scarce. Research carried out from the management perspective is even scarcer. The articles by Hoyle and Oldham in *Reader 1* indicate what is available. Most studies, as you will see, have been carried out by sociologists. Now there are distinct differences between the management and sociological perspectives, and you should be sensitive to these in your reading. Before discussing the two articles by Hoyle and Oldham let us briefly state the differences between the management and sociological points of view.

'Managerialism' is often regarded by sociologists with a certain lofty scorn. This is returned with interest by the contempt in which many educational practitioners hold sociological theory. These extreme attitudes are illustrated in Figure 2.

Figure 2   Management–Sociology Stereotypes

	Management Perspective	Sociological Perspective
Intellectual Level	'Lightweight'	'Heavyweight'
Purpose	Prescriptive ↓ Action	Descriptive ↓ Theory
Values	Efficiency	Value-free

Figure 2 is a parody, if you like, of opposing views. Let us adjust the balance.

Intellectual Level

It is not true that all writers from the management perspective are 'lightweight'. Messrs March and Simon, for example, exhibit ample intellectual substance. It may be that such popular management authors as Drucker slide easily from empirical report to the pronouncement of empty axioms. But also, some sociologists appear to mistake dense prose and abstract (often confused) concepts as marks of intellectual quality.

Purpose

It is true that management writing is primarily addressed to managers who have pragmatic interests. To that extent it is bound to be prescriptive. But it is also true that sociological writing is addressed to sociologists whose aims are not always those of the disinterested and co-operative construction of theories. Competing sociological theories too are prescriptive. They claim: '*this* is the way to understand social phenomena'. Both perspectives have the provision of understanding as a common purpose. What the understanding leads to in practical terms only reflects the fact that managers and (academic) sociologists have different jobs.

Values

Sociologists are apt to be unsympathetic to and suspicious of the values of managers. 'Manipulation' is hinted at darkly. If the management perspective is to be used, says Oldham, 'it is particularly important that the underlying assumptions and values are made explicit and subjected to rigorous scrutiny'.[40] The same rigorous scrutiny ought to apply to the sociological perspective. No sociologist, for example, who was also a Marxist, could justly claim that his work was 'value-free'.

It is inappropriate here to embark on a detailed discussion of the nature of 'theory' and the question of whether it can be purely descriptive – i.e. incapable of being used to validate 'ought' statements. The aim is simply to indicate some attitudinal differences between the management and sociological perspectives of which you should be aware when you read studies on organizations.

The articles by Hoyle and Oldham are set reading for the unit. Both concern empirical research into schools as organizations and both also discuss ways in which theory enters into research decisions. The papers are sociologically oriented – hence the preceding rather defensive digression on differences between the sociological and management perspectives.

Hoyle commences with a valuable account of the recent historical development of the study of schools as organizations. He then goes on to point out the multi-dimensional qualities of schools and the necessity, therefore, of the researcher making certain choices. Ten possible choices are put forward, each one of which Hoyle briefly analyses. In the second half of the article he considers some of the (admittedly few) empirical studies which have been carried out. He groups these into case studies and comparative studies. Finally, he lists the topics Counselling, Authority, and School–community relations as possible areas for fruitful research. Research on these could refer to relevant American work and could raise important methodological issues.

Oldham gives a semi-autobiographical account of the way in which she designed a research project in a school undergoing comprehensive reorganization. After a general introduction she discusses her selection of a theoretical viewpoint and choice of approach. Her initial choice to study a single school instead of carrying out a comparative study was influenced by the Hoyle article. The theoretical framework was adopted after spending some time in the school and developing an awareness of the issues involved. This turned out to be the 'Action' frame of reference defined by Silverman, which was preferred to the Systems approach. Oldham's provisional conclusions are that the choice of theoretical framework was justified and that the research tended to illustrate the need for more investigation into the features differentiating schools from other types of organization.

In Activity 4 you will be asked to read the Hoyle and Oldham articles.

Summary

2.18 In this section we have:

Discussed the reasons for studying organizations: managers in education have pragmatic reasons.

Defined the concept of 'organization': over-general, over-specific or highly programmatic definitions can cause problems.

Illustrated the diversity and conflicting nature of organization theory: we need to form a synthesis relevant to management in education.

Argued that any worth-while synthesis should be based on the distinctive features of schools as organizations and the management role.

Attempted to elucidate the distinctive features of schools by using a four-variable framework – goals, technology, participation and values.

Discussed the management role in the school and mentioned six typical problems expressed by heads.

Sketched the differences of attitude between the management and sociological perspectives and outlined the two readings on research into schools as organizations.

Activity 4

Hoyle and Oldham readings.

You should now read the Hoyle and Oldham papers in *Reader 1* (Reading 2.2, pp. 85–108, and Reading 4.6, pp. 366–80). As noted above, there is a certain common ground between these. Both, for example, are concerned with choice of theoretical perspective. In your reading look especially for the ways in which these writers deal with the justification of such choices.

The purpose of this activity is to enable you to see more clearly the range of available modes of investigation and theory. The readings convey the wider academic perspective on the study of schools as organizations.

You should allow about one hour for this Activity.

3 THEORIES OF ORGANIZATION: A REVIEW

3.1   This section reviews some main approaches to organization theory.
Classical Theory
Bureaucracy
Human Relations
Systems Theory
are chosen for review as having had the most influence on management thought
and practice. Some of the ideas in the above 'schools of thought' will already be
familiar to you from Unit 1. Lastly we shall look at
Phenomenology
as a radical alternative to the above approaches.

After working through the previous section of this unit you should now be armed
with a rough critical framework based on your own experience–perceptions of
schools as organizations. The aim here is to enable you to develop your views by
taking into account the concepts and perspectives of others, as expressed in the
theories reviewed. There is not the space in a single unit to carry out a completely
systematic review, for example by examining *all* the variables and example
problems (paragraphs 2.9 and 2.16) against the selected theoretical perspectives.
There will necessarily remain judgements, connections and questions for you to
formulate and work on during later parts of the course and in your wider reading.
Developing this kind of synthesis is a continuing process.

3.2   It is important to realize that 'Not only the organizational procedures of schools
but also the characteristic approaches to the problems of school management have
deep historical roots'[41]; and also that 'Organizational systems are *cultural* answers
to the problems human beings find in achieving their collective ends.'[42]

Although the writers whose work we shall consider often present a 'timeless' view
of organizations, their theories are likewise creatures of particular cultures and
periods. The cultural aspects of management in education will be dealt with later
in the course, and we shall not anticipate the discussion here. But before going on
to review the selected approaches you should read the following historical note
which describes the origins of just one approach to the management of
educational organizations. This approach – the 'efficient production' model – has
affinities with classical theory and is still a major element in the organizational
thinking of many school administrators. It is included not only for general interest
value but also as an antidote to the commonly expressed view of the supposed
recent emergence and extrinsic nature of management principles in education.

Historical Note

3.3   Bennett declares: 'In comparison with developments in the industrial and
commercial sectors, management principles have come relatively recently to
schools and other educational organizations.'[43] Nothing could be further from the
truth. It *is* the case that formal management training in education is largely a
phenomenon of the last two decades, but the application of business-management
principles in popular education can be traced back at least to the early nineteenth
century. P. J. Miller provides a fascinating short account of those origins (see note
41). The subscription charity school, he points out, followed the commercial
model of the joint stock company as an operation dependent on the raising of
resources from many individuals and the handing over of management to a chosen
few. School managers, like their counterparts in industry, were expected to deal
with limited resources and to be economical with cash, labour and time. These
concerns were responsible for the enthusiasm for the 'monitorial system'
associated with the names of Joseph Lancaster and Andrew Bell. This system was
a direct transfer to education of the newly discovered factory production methods.

It was essentially no more than a methodical routine for teaching children to teach others through the repetition of lessons. It was based upon specified objectives and procedures which were distinguished only by their complexity and unutterable dullness.

Bell wrote in 1807:

> Machinery has been contrived for spinning twenty skeins of silk, and twenty hanks of cotton, where one was spun before; but no contrivance has been sought for, or devised, that twenty children may be educated in moral and religious principles with the same facility and expense, as one was taught before.[44]

The monitorial system whereby one teacher could teach vast numbers of children by repeating lessons through relays of monitors was just such a 'contrivance'. The enthusiasm for the system is exemplified by Coleridge's descriptions of it as 'an incomparable machine', a 'vast moral steam engine'.[45] Thomas Bernard wrote in 1809:

> The grand principle of Dr. Bell's system is the division of labour applied to intellectual purposes. . . . it is the division of labour in his schools that leaves the master the easy task of directing the movements of the whole machine, instead of toiling ineffectually at a single part. The principle of manufactories, and in schools is the same.[46]

Similar ideas were developed by Jeremy Bentham in a splendid mixture of embryonic management theory and ethical utilitarianism published under the title *Chrestomathia* in 1816. He elucidated thirty-eight principles of school management applicable, as he thought, to all branches of intellectual instruction. Anticipating Fayol by a hundred years, he arranged these principles in five categories concerning the most effective placement and utilization of teaching personnel, preserving discipline, keeping management-control information, ensuring that instructional objectives were attained, and finally doing all this with 'the union of the maximum of despatch with the maximum of uniformity; thereby proportionably shortening the time employed in the acquisition of the proposed body of instruction, and increasing the number of pupils made to acquire it, by the same teachers, at the same time'.

Chrestomathia, in fact, was a detailed prescription for a novel kind of day school, to be run on secular lines, and also an exposition of the principles of management in accordance with which it could be conducted. It was to be a school for the children of the 'middling and higher ranks of life', but the Chrestomathic blueprint would serve for the conduct of all educational institutions. The teaching, pupils' progress, incentives, rewards, discipline and internal government were all carefully planned to ensure that the objectives were achieved. Bentham, James Mill, Francis Place and others were active in seeking to establish a Chrestomathic School in London. A scheme was drawn up and a site in Bentham's own garden at Queen's Square Place was agreed upon. However, in the end the proposals foundered. A similar school was set up about the same time by the Hill brothers at Hazelwood, Birmingham, and Jeremy Bentham was in correspondence with Rowland Hill about it; another school was founded on the same lines by the Hill brothers at Bruce Castle, Tottenham. It is also of some interest that the physical plans for the Chrestomathic School, and indeed the whole system of management, which reached an advanced stage before their abandonment, bear a strong resemblance to Bentham's design for a penal establishment, the 'Panopticon'.

The 'management' of elementary schools on the lines of the monitorial system did not change materially before the middle of the nineteenth century. Robert Owen was also an innovator in the field of elementary education at this time. He was interested in both industrial and educational management at New Lanark, where he owned and ran a cotton mill from 1800 to 1824 and simultaneously directed the activities of a school which he attached to his factory for the education of the children of the operatives up to the age of ten. In his 'Address to the Inhabitants of New Lanark' (January 1816), Owen claimed that he had been successful in both enterprises. He advocated wholly secular education for the New Lanark and other pupils, and he laid great emphasis upon the 'formation of character', in which process he believed environmental influences played an all-important part. Such men as Lancaster, Bell, Bentham and Owen would have been at home in the situation after 1862 when, under the terms of the Revised Code, a system of 'payment by results' was introduced into schools. (This was bitterly criticized by Matthew Arnold, among others, then an Inspector of Schools.) They would have thrived during the first thirty years of this century in American schools systems influenced by the business efficiency cult,[47] or again in Arkansas during the school year 1970–71 when the US Office of Economic Opportunity spent \$7.2m on trying out performance contracting – which the OEO concluded to be a failure.[48]

At the risk of labouring the point this historical note should have established that at least one set of management–organizational principles has a long history in education. There is, sadly, little evidence that present-day enthusiasts for the varying styles of management approaches in education are sensitive to the lessons which might be learned from the past.

In retrospect it is easy to see the historical connections between the growth of nineteenth-century factory production methods and corresponding innovations in educational organizations. The social, political, economic and industrial changes of the present also have a (two-way) influence on our educational organizations. This suggests questions in organization theory. For example, is classical theory especially relevant to organizations in countries undergoing fast industrialization? Or, what is the connection between the growth of computer use in the last two decades and the fashion for systems theory in organization? In the following review of organization theories you should try, wherever possible through your wider reading, to set them in their social, historical and cultural context.

Classical Theory

3.4   'Scientific management will mean, for the employers and the workmen who adopt it, the elimination of almost all causes for dispute and disagreement between them.' – F. W. Taylor

'To manage is to forecast and plan, to organize, to command, to co-ordinate and to control.' – Henri Fayol

'I am convinced that a logical scheme of organization, a structure based on principles, which take priority over personalities, is in the long run far better both for the morale of an undertaking as a whole and for the happiness of individuals, than the attempt to build one's organization round persons.' – L. F. Urwick

F. W. Taylor

In classical theory we include 'scientific management' (the 'engineering' or 'production' approach of Unit 1, paragraph 3.3) and administrative management theory. The former is especially associated with F. W. Taylor, the latter with Henri Fayol and in England with Urwick and Sheldon. You should now read quickly through Chapters 24, 25 and 26 of Hicks. These give an adequate account of classical theory, so it is unnecessary to add to this in our text. (For other brief versions see Massie[49] and Pugh.[50])

Classical theory, as Owens says, 'was structured around two fundamental ideas: *motivation,* the explanation of why a person participates in an organization, and *organization,* specifically, techniques of dividing up specialized tasks and the various levels of authority.' Motivation in classical theory is relatively simple: the view is of 'economic man'. People work for money to meet basic needs, and beyond that because they want a profit.

> In dealing with organization, classical theorists emphasize division of labor, breaking down the total job into its specialized steps and processes whereby each worker becomes highly skilled in his special task. The organization is structured according to a plan that organizes all the small specialized steps into a pattern, thus assuring that the total task of the organization will be accomplished. In the classical view, not only is the detailed plan vital, but strong central control and careful supervision at every step are essential to keep things coordinated. When diagrammed, this type of organization takes on a pyramidal form with a strong executive in control at the top and subordinate executives in successive lower layers of the organization, none of whom has more people under his direct authority than he can personally supervise. The aspects of organization stressed by classical theory – specialization of work, span of control, the pyramid of control, and the clearly segmented divisions – have come to connote what is today known as *formal organization*.[51]

The simple 'economic man' view of motivation has had its impact on schools by way of the occasional fashions for payment-by-results schemes. It is probable, though, that the organizational aspects of classical theory are more relevant to education. The image of a school as an organization which we would gain from classical theory would 'emphasize concepts such as authority, a clear-cut hierarchy with centralized control, a definite division of functions and responsibilities, and orderly channels of communication.'[52] Many heads of schools and university administrators in the author's experience have just such an image of the educational organization.

Now although classical theory is nowadays often ignored by social scientists, the following are possible reasons to commend it for our attention:

(a) Although

the classical school was derided for presenting 'principles' that were really only proverbs, all the resources of organizational research and theory today have not managed to substitute better principles (or proverbs) for those ridiculed.

(b) Also

these principles, which amount to pious directives to 'plan ahead', pay attention to coordination, refrain from wasting time on established routine functions, and devote managerial energies to the exceptional cases that come up, served management very well. As obvious as 'plan ahead' sounds, it took a lot of saying in the 1920s, for business rarely did any planning. (Today the injunctions parade under the name 'Management by Objectives [MBO]', and in more mathematical terms, PERT ['Program Evaluation and Review Technique'].) It was also quite a struggle to separate the chief executive (often the founder, or his relative) from routine affairs – to get him to delegate authority and deal only with the exceptions. It still is.

(c) . . . a successful and durable business of management consulting and an endless series of successful books rest upon the basic principles of the classical management school. These principles have worked and are still working, for they addressed themselves to very real problems of management, problems more pressing than those advanced by social science.[53]

(d) Even though managers in schools and elsewhere are reluctant to subscribe overtly to the classical approach, the assumptions and ideologies underlying their actions are often those of classical theory. The classical paradigm remains powerful and pervasive.

(e) The organizational concepts of classical theory are familiar to many educational administrators; for example:

Line and Staff
Unity of Command
Span of Control
Delegation of Responsibility.

The three reasons (a)–(c) adduced by Perrow above are perhaps contentious. The last two reasons would be more widely accepted.

In assessing the relevance of classical theory to the management of educational organizations we are faced with the difficult problem of trying to disentangle two interwoven strands.

One is the attempt at an abstract description of the elements of formal organization, the other a set of practical guides to action in the design and management of organizations. The method of exposition these writers employed was to draw upon their own practical experience and that of others to define the salient features of efficient organizations, and then to describe methods for the design and management of efficient organizations and some of the problems to be solved in the process.[54]

Now the organizations where men like Fayol and Urwick gained their experience were in the fields of industry or public administration. We are asking, therefore, how *transferable* their practical guides to action are. Do these notions really fit schools as we know them? In assessing this you may like to consider the following critical points:

(a) In the classical view organizations exist for purposes; they have objectives. Efficiency begins with defining objectives precisely, deciding what has to be done to achieve the objectives, assigning people to carry out the necessary activities, reformulating objectives as necessary, and so on. We have argued already that objectives in education are, to say the least, problematic.

34

(b) How adequate is the engineering analogy in describing schools as organizations? Would an organic analogy be more appropriate?

(c) The standard criticisms of classical theory are that the 'economic man' view of motivation is too simple and that the informal aspects of organizations are ignored. If these criticisms are valid for industrial organizations they may apply even more strongly to educational organizations.

(d) As academic theory the classical school has long been out of the game. There is little chance of fresh insights and understanding from this source.

But despite the above points, classical theorists have bequeathed a number of concepts which remain part of our apparatus for describing organizations, and much of the ideology of classical theory (though of earlier origins) remains in present management thought and practice in schools. You have then the rudiments of a for-and-against case. It is up to you to take it further. During the course you will encounter in texts and broadcasts a number of pronouncements on educational management which could be derived directly from classical theory. Your assessment of classical theory will enable you to slot these where they belong. You should also remind yourself of the material in Unit 2, and consider the extent to which management at Sidney Stringer has departed from the precepts common to classical theory, and the apparent reasons for any departure you observe.

Before leaving classical theorists of organization let us consider one device usually associated with these writers – the formal organization chart. Organization charts are a device used to solve one of the problems posed in paragraph 2.16 above, i.e. 'How to communicate the (often changing) organization structure to outsiders and those within the school'. A simple formal organization chart aiming to state differences of function and authority is shown in Figure 3.

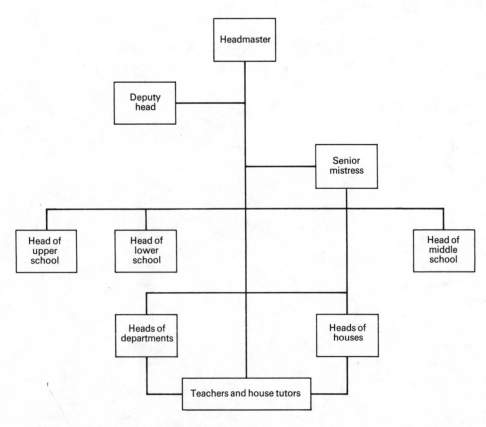

Figure 3   An example of school organization

A slightly more sophisticated version might show line and staff differences in addition, as in Figure 4.

35

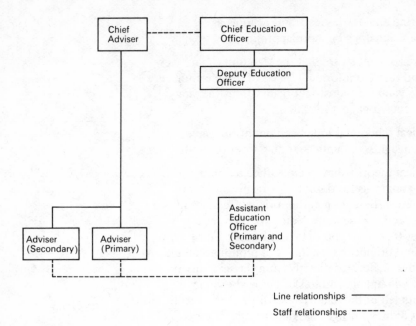

Figure 4 A section of the organization chart for a large Local Education Authority

Line relationships ——————
Staff relationships – – – – –

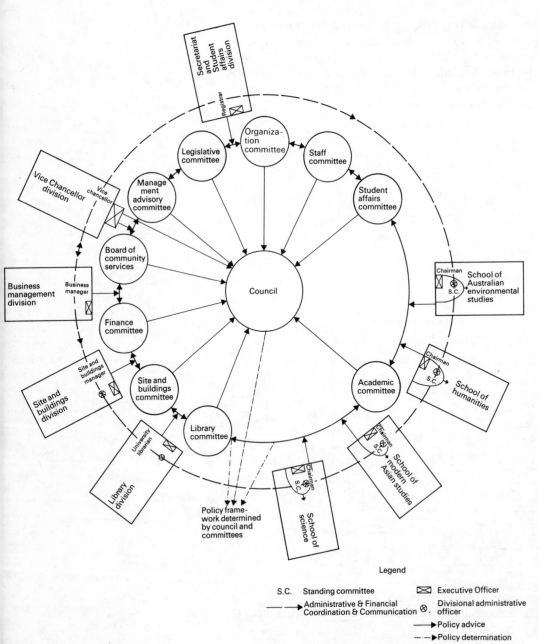

Legend

S.C.   Standing committee

———▶ Administrative & Financial Coordination & Communication

———▶ Policy advice

–·–·–▶ Policy determination

⊠ Executive Officer

⊗ Divisional administrative officer

Figure 5 Griffith University, Brisbane, Queensland, Australia Organizational Structure (March 1973) (Showing Policy and Administrative Relationships)

It is not, of course, necessary to draw formal organization charts as hierarchical trees. Figure 5, produced by a new Australian university, features in my 'black museum' of formal organization charts. It adopts a circular format, presumably to avoid the 'fearful symmetry' and authoritarian overtones of the traditional variety. It also tries to show lines of policy and communication. You may form your own conclusions as to how successful this formidable diagram is likely to be in communicating the realities of organizational life at Griffith University.

It is unfortunately true that most diagrams which purport to describe the structure of an organization fail conspicuously. The informal dimensions are too complex to be included. Attempts to make charts more comprehensive by including lines of communication, policy, and so on, usually result in the creation of topological tangles.

Even single dimensions of organizations turn out to be surprisingly difficult to represent in chart form. Figure 6 below is intended to show lines of communication within the Open University, and is taken from the current handbook *What is the Open University?* It has obvious faults. For example, it would appear that although students address queries to tutors and counsellors they do not receive replies! It is perhaps unfair to pick on a figure with omissions which are possibly accidental, but you might speculate on just how many extra lines and arrows would be needed if the figure were to show the actual lines of communication which exist.

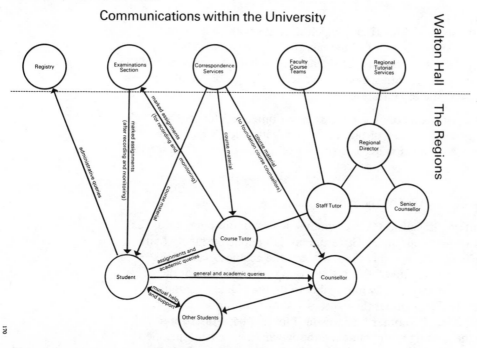

Figure 6   Communications within the Open University

It will not have required special powers of perception on your part to have noticed a certain antipathy here to formal organization charts. To correct any possible bias you may like to examine the organization chart of your own school or other employing organization, if such a document exists. Start by asking yourself the question: What do the lines (vertical and horizontal) actually mean? Then ask: What significance does the arrangement of boxes about the page have?

If you get further (and you will not with most organization charts), ask: Does this really represent the distribution of authority and function in the organization? Finally: Why should I not burn this chart? (If after this exercise you would like to study organization charts further, Chapter 17 of Hicks deals with the topic. On page 275 of Hicks you will find some questions on charts.) The Sidney Stringer documentary material in Unit 2 (see Document 13) contains several diagrams which aim to represent the organization of that school. You can estimate how far these succeed in avoiding some of the disadvantages of traditional varieties of charts.

Bureaucracy

3.5 Consider the following 'classic' quotations:

Max Weber

> The decisive reason for the advance of bureaucratic organization has always been its purely technical superiority over any other form of organization. The fully developed bureaucratic mechanism compares with other organizations exactly as does the machine with the non-mechanical modes of production. – Max Weber

> . . . a system of rational–legal authority can only operate through imposing and enforcing with relative efficiency, seriously frustrating limits on many important human interests, interests which either operate independently of particular institutions, in any society, or are generated by the strains inherent in the particular structure itself. One source of such strain is the segregation of roles, and of the corresponding authority to use influence over others and over non-human resources, which is inherent in the functionally limited sphere of office. There are always tendencies to stretch the sanctioned limits of official authority to take in ranges of otherwise 'personal' interests. In other words this form of institutionalization involves a kind of 'abstraction' of a part of the human individual from the concrete whole which is in a certain sense 'unreal' and hence can only be maintained by continual discipline. – Talcott Parsons

You should now read Chapter 28 of Hicks, which introduces the concept of bureaucracy and gives a short account of bureaucratic organizations. Hicks concentrates on the dysfunctional aspects of bureaucracy. In Unit 1, paragraphs 4.4 to 4.9 also discuss bureaucracy, with special reference to the problems of the professional in a bureaucratic organization.

The notion of bureaucracy in a theoretical context is attributed to Weber. There is, however, a common pejorative view of bureaucratic organization which is much older. Dickens anticipates Parkinson in this extract from *Little Dorrit,* Chapter 10.

The Concept of Bureaucracy (Pre-Weberian)

> The Circumlocution Office was (as everybody knows without being told) the most important Department under Government. No public business of any kind could possibly be done at any time, without the acquiescence of the Circumlocution Office. Its finger was in the largest public pie, and in the smallest public tart. It was equally impossible to do the plainest right and to undo the plainest wrong, without the express authority of the Circumlocution Office. If another Gunpowder Plot had been discovered half an hour before the lighting of the match, nobody would have been justified in saving the parliament until there had been half a score of boards, half a bushel of minutes, several sacks of official memoranda, and a family-vault full of ungrammatical correspondence, on the part of the Circumlocution Office.

> This glorious establishment had been early in the field, when the one sublime principle involving the difficult art of governing a country was first distinctly revealed to statesmen. It has been foremost to study that bright revelation, and to carry its shining influence through the whole of the official proceedings. Whatever was required to be done, the Circumlocution Office was beforehand with all the public departments in the art of perceiving – HOW NOT TO DO IT. . . .

> Because the Circumlocution Office went on mechanically, every day, keeping this wonderful, all-sufficient wheel of statemanship, How not to do it, in motion. Because the Circumlocution Office was down upon any ill-advised public servant who was going to do it, or who appeared to be by any surprising accident in remote danger of doing it, with a minute, and a memorandum, and a letter of instructions, that extinguished him. It was this

spirit of national efficiency in the Circumlocution Office that had gradually led to its having something to do with everything. Mechanicians, natural philosophers, soldiers, sailors, petitioners, memorialists, people with grievances people who wanted to prevent grievances, people who wanted to redress grievances, jobbing people, jobbed people, people who couldn't

THE REGISTRAR-GENERAL'S OFFICE—THE SEARCH ROOM.

get rewarded for merit, and people who couldn't get punished for demerit, were all indiscriminately tucked up under the foolscap paper of the Circumlocution Office.

Numbers of people were lost in the Circumlocution Office. Unfortunates with wrongs, or with projects for the general welfare (and they had better have had wrongs at first, than have taken that bitter English recipe for certainly getting them), who in slow lapse of time and agony had passed safely through other public departments; who, according to rule, had been bullied in this, over-reached by that, and evaded by the other; got referred at last to the Circumlocution Office, and never reappeared in the light of day. Boards sat upon them, secretaries minuted upon them, commissioners gabbled about them, clerks registered, entered, checked, and ticked them off, and they melted away. In short, all the business of the country went through the Circumlocution Office, except the business that never came out of it; and *its* name was Legion.

Weber though, writing at a period of increasing industrialization and the growth of government departments, saw bureaucratic administration as a necessity for coping with the organizational problems which arise in large organizations. He foresaw a historical trend towards bureaucracy.

The characteristics of bureaucracy are:

(a) Organizational tasks are distributed among the various posts as official duties.

(b) The posts are organized into a hierarchical authority-structure.

(c) A formally established system of rules and regulations governs official decisions and actions.

39

(d) Officials are expected to assume an impersonal orientation in their contacts with clients and with other officials.

(e) Employment by the organization constitutes a career for officials.

(f) Lines of communication are maintained by an administrative staff.

Clearly bureaucratization is a matter of degree. Schools occupy a position on the scale somewhere between government departments at the highly bureaucratized end and, say, a therapy group at the opposite extreme.

It has been suggested that nowadays schools are moving further towards the bureaucratic ideal type. One reason may be that the average size of schools has increased, partly owing to comprehensive reorganization. Another reason may be the increase in supportive and administrative units both within the school and outside – resource centres, career guidance, and so on.[55] For management in education it is important to ask: What are the possible dysfunctional results of increased bureaucratization of schools?

Hicks gives a racy account on pp. 432–8 of 'avoiding responsibility', 'the buck-passer', 'the ostrich', 'hoarding authority', and so on. No doubt you will find examples of these from your own experience.

Here we shall single out two possible bureaucratic dysfunctions which seem especially relevant to schools as organizations:

(a) Client dissatisfaction;

(b) Value-system conflicts.

Figure 7 depicts the processes leading to client dissatisfaction.

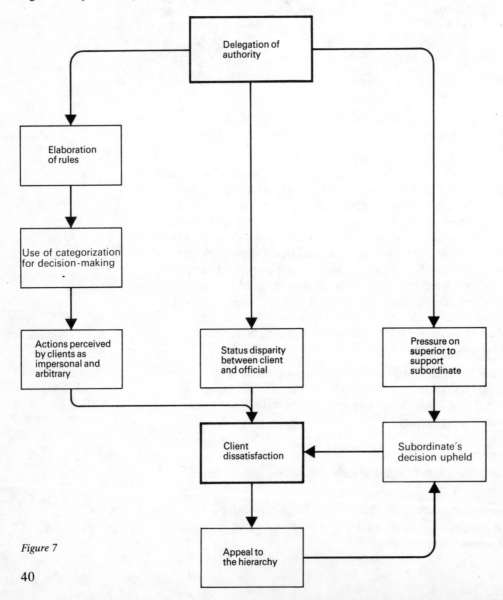

Figure 7

40

Bobbitt writes:

Depersonalization

In traditional theories, the treatment of clients has two characteristics that lead to client dissatisfaction. First, the stress on *depersonalization* leads to clients being categorized and treated by the application of general, abstract rules, without regard for individual needs and situations. The depersonalized behavior was considered functional because it prevented emotional involvement with the client's problems and tended to promote consistency in behavior throughout the organization. The client, however, usually sees his case as special and objects to such categorical treatment. He is not satisfied with impersonal treatment of problems that are of great personal significance to him. The college senior who is closed out of a course he needs for graduation is exasperated by the simple explanation that his registration card was thirty-second in a class that closes when enrollment reaches thirty. He is further disturbed if he knows that the room is large enough for 32 people, and the pedagogy employed in the course will accommodate more students. In other words, the client is likely to be particularly dissatisfied if he perceives the rule on which his treatment is based as both inappropriate to his particular situation and arbitrary.

Second, conflict with clients may be created when the bureaucrat who speaks as a representative of the power and prestige of the entire organization occupies a relatively low-level position in the hierarchy. The careful and thorough establishment of rules by the organization makes it possible to delegate substantial authority to persons far down in the organization structure. This is theoretically efficient for the organization because potentially complex problems can then be routinely handled by persons with relatively slight training and commonplace abilities, who can be employed inexpensively. In effect, it is equivalent to task specialization in the shop. The senior student who has been closed out of a required course frequently finds himself appealing to a departmental clerk or secretary who may herself be younger than he, perhaps a recent high school graduate with only a few weeks' experience.

If the unfortunate student gets past the secretary to a higher authority, he may still be disappointed because the pressures on the person in the position to which he is appealing are to hold firm on the original decision, in order to support the subordinate who has been instructed to operate within the rules. It becomes difficult to get a decision reversed once it has been made.[56]

This quotation and Figure 7 require no additional comment.

Value-system conflicts

The conflict we have in mind is that between the bureaucrat (administrator–manager) and the professional (teacher) – see Unit 1, paragraph 4.8. Conflicts can arise because, it is said:

(a) The bureaucrat's foremost responsibilities are to represent and promote the interests of his organization but the professional is bound by a norm of service and a code of ethics to represent the welfare and interests of his clients.

(b) The authority of the bureaucratic official rests on a legal contract backed by formal sanctions, but the authority of the professional is rooted in his acknowledged technical expertise.

(c) The bureaucrat's decisions are expected to be governed by disciplined compliance with directives from superiors, whereas the professional's decisions are to be governed by internalized professional standards.

(d) When the decision of a bureaucrat is questioned the final judgement as to whether he is right or not is a prerogative of management, but when a decision of a professional is questioned the right of reviewing its correctness is reserved to his professional-colleague group.

41

Figure 8 shows the origins of value-system conflicts in the bureaucracy.

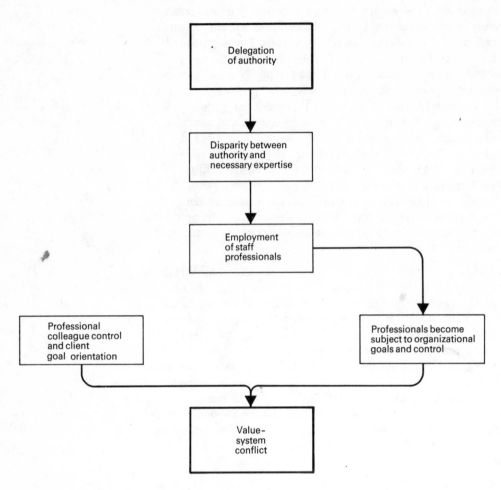

Figure 8

Figure 9 below shows the respective orientations of the professional (for example the teacher) and the bureaucrat (for example the administrator) in simplified form.

Figure 9[57]

Orientation Behavior Characteristic	Professional	Bureaucratic
Decision standards	Body of professional knowledge	Rules and regulations of the organization
Expertness	Specific to the knowledge area	Specific to the knowledge area
Relation to clients	Emotional neutrality	Emotional neutrality
Status	Achieved by performance	Achieved by performance
Objective	Client's interest	Self or organizational interest
Control	Colleague group	Organizational hierarchy

No prescriptions are available for dealing with the problems of client dissatisfaction or value-system conflict. Our suggestion is simply that such problems do exist in schools and that an understanding of the bureaucratic organization as developed by Perrow (1972), Anderson (1968) (see note of further reading below) and others is possibly of some help. Although the theory of bureaucracy is primarily academic rather than practical, there does seem to be potential relevance here to real problems in educational organizations.

In conclusion we note that the virtues of bureaucracies are well known. According to Owens, they are 'efficient', 'predictable', 'impersonal' and 'fast' in the sense that 'uniform rules are impartially applied to process thousands of cases quickly' (see op. cit., note 51, p. 60). That is not to say that all bureaucracies are equally effective, or that they are constant in their state of health over time. Criticisms include the encouragement of over-conformity, and lack of recognition of the informal organization and the individual personality. Bureaucracies are not noted for rapid communication or for innovation.

Some of the limitations of bureaucracy as a theory of organization are shared with classical theory. They derive from the treatment of organizations as deterministic, i.e. the outcomes of organizational processes are treated as if they were completely predictable. In fact, unanticipated consequences occur in every organization. Some of these tend to be dysfunctional in that they do not contribute to the purposes served by the organization. We have noted two of these – client dissatisfaction and value-system conflict – which may occur in the school.

For further reading see Perrow (1972), and specifically from the educational aspect, Anderson (1968) and Bidwell (1965).[58]

Human Relations

3.6 Consider the following statements:

[An organization] is a social system, a system of cliques, grapevines, informal status systems, rituals and a mixture of logical, non-logical and illogical behaviour. – Elton Mayo

It is my hypothesis that the present organizational strategies developed and used by administrators (be they industrial, educational, religious, governmental or trade union) lead to human and organizational decay. It is also my hypothesis that this need not be so. – Chris Argyris

Theory X
The average human being has an inherent dislike of work and will avoid it if he can. Because of this human characteristic of dislike of work, most people must be coerced, controlled, directed and threatened with punishment to get them to put forth adequate effort toward the achievement of organizational objectives.
The average human being prefers to be directed, wishes to avoid responsibility, has relatively little ambition, wants security above all.

Theory Y
The expenditure of physical and mental effort in work is as natural as play or rest. Man will exercise self-direction and self-control in the service of objectives to which he is committed.
The average human being learns under proper conditions not only to accept, but to seek responsibility. – Douglas McGregor[59]

You should now read the brief summary of the work of the human-relations
theorists given in Hicks (set book), pp. 374–7. The subject arrangement of Hicks
does not lead easily to gaining a quick appreciation of the central ideas in the
human-relations school. Chapters 18 and 19 are perhaps the best starting points.
After reading those you can then decide which parts of Hicks's Section II,
'Human Behavior – The Basic Resource in Organizations', are relevant. In *Reader
1* all the articles in Section 3, 'Individuals and Organizations', bear on the
human-relations issues in one way or another. Directly useful is the piece by
Argyris, 'The Individual and Organization: Some Problems of Mutual
Adjustment' (Reading 3.5, pp. 233–52), which must hold the record for the most
anthologized paper in the whole organizational field. Obviously you cannot be
expected to read all this material in the context of working this one unit. You
should, however, try to cover at least the Argyris article and Chapters 18 and 19
of Hicks.

Although the human-relations school – if we take it to include the later refinements
and contributions of behavioural researchers – is the most flourishing and dominant
in organization theory, it is not without its critics. Strauss, for example, has
systematically questioned the notions of 'harmony', 'the hierarchy of needs',
'conflict resolution', and 'participation'.[60]

It is not easy to criticize ideas which seem to carry with them an aura of such moral
virtue. As Perrow has remarked, to oppose human-relations views is like knocking
motherhood and promoting sin. Yet there is a difference between fostering
organizational hygiene and participation and allowing the exercise of legitimate
self-assertion, which is a *political* resource.[61]

Perrow asserts:

> One may treat a slave humanely, and even ask his opinion regarding matters
> he is more familiar with than the master. But to transform his basic
> dependency and this presumption of his incompetence with regard to his own
> interests, there must be an institutional order or public process whereby the
> opportunity and capacity for legitimate self-assertion is guaranteed. Such a
> political process does not mean conflict and struggle as such, but a setting for
> ordered controversy and accommodation.[62]

At a different level one suspects that the ideals of democratic management based on human-relations concepts may sometimes be upheld in bad faith. Owens writes:

> At times, administrators wishing to do the 'right' thing (i.e. be democratic administrators) would often attempt to decrease the visibility of their power in an honest desire to be a democratic not authoritarian. Yet the power was still there, although perhaps momentarily hidden, but it would appear and vanish unpredictably and rapidly. In many situations teachers felt that their positions were not 'democratic' at all, but they were being manoeuvred into agreeing to decisions which generally had been arrived at previously. This feeling of being manipulated by a clever administrator who knew clearly where he was heading has probably contributed to the cynicism and suspicion among teachers that are commonly encountered in our schools. The notion of democratic administration has proven to be a difficult one to accept in conjunction with the realities of organizational life in schools.[63]

Did you perhaps detect anything of the problem Owens mentions in the case of the Sidney Stringer School and Community College?

Despite these criticisms, human-relations views are based on a better understanding of motivation than the 'economic man' view of classical theory, which Mayo described as the 'rabble hypothesis'. And the views packaged as 'Shared Decision-Making', 'MBO', 'Grid Theory' or 'Organization Development' (see Unit 6 on OD) have a growing circulation in education. However, the perennial dichotomies – Theory X–Theory Y, Mechanistic–Organismic, and so on – reflect the continuing dilemma for the practising manager of reconciling the seeming incompatibilities of rationalistic and humanistic approaches. Argyris dramatically concludes his article in *Reader 1:*

> This dilemma between individual needs and organization demands is a basic, continual problem posing an eternal challenge to the leader. How is it possible to create an organization in which the individuals may obtain optimum expression and, simultaneously, in which the organization itself may obtain optimum satisfaction of its demands? Here lies a fertile field for future research in organizational behaviour.[64]

Systems Theory
by Harry Gray

3.7 Chapter 30 of Hicks explains the general theory of open systems from a management standpoint. You should read this now.

The virtue of systems theory is that it illustrates the relationships that exist among objects or ideas: it shows how part relates to part. At its core is the idea that systems exist within an environment to which they are inextricably bound. So far as human behaviour is concerned, the concept of a system has disadvantages if the analogy is expressed too mechanically, but systems theory has a persistent element of clarity that many researchers and theorists find useful in developing ideas about organizations.

Hicks defines a system as 'a set of interrelated, interdependent, or interacting elements. It is an organized or complex whole; a combination of things forming a unitary whole.' Open-systems theory serves as the basis for management techniques such as corporate planning and operations research, and is essential for any analysis of local and national government. In the case of education, open-systems theory can depict, say, the relationship between a school and the local education authority. Thus the local education authority sets up the school, maintains it, recruits teachers, pupils, and ancillary staff, and implements the educational policy of the government and the elected representatives on the local council. The LEA mediates in some way between parents and employers on the one hand and the school on the other. However, the school is also a sub-system of other systems, such as the teaching profession, the teacher-training programme, a religious denomination, a distinctive local culture (for example a Welsh-speaking area) and so on. The open-systems concept enables us to show these relationships in both diagrammatic and conceptual terms.

For example, the idea of the community school is sustained by an open-systems view of the place of the school in society. Instead of viewing the school as part of (e.g.) the grammar-school system, where 'grammar-school' values were paramount, the school is seen as part of a local social system and derives its purposes and ethos from an understanding of that situation. Of course, other 'systems' still have influence, such as the examination system, opportunities for employment, or the social and academic aspirations of parents, but at the centre of the idea of the community school is the understanding that no social institution can work satisfactorily if it is cut off from the social and economic environment from which it arises and in which it functions.

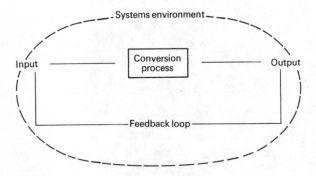

Figure 10   A simple Systems Model

The simple systems representation given in Figure 10 shows how the 'inputs' into a system undergo some processes of 'conversion' into a product or 'output', and the effects of the 'output' on the environment are monitored so as to modify future 'inputs'. Schools can be thought of as places where the 'process' of education works on the minds and personalities of all the members (including teachers), and the 'product' is the effect of this educational process, which will thus be qualitative as well as quantitative. The 'feedback' loop represents the information on which the educational process is modified to better provide for the needs of pupils and students entering the school system. Hence, future changes in, say, vocational opportunities are catered for in terms of new entrants into the school. In schools the feedback process may centre on decisions made in the staff meeting when, for instance, examination results are received and new syllabuses adapted in response, or when new reading schemes are adopted to improve the number of seven-year-olds with high reading ability. No school can be closed entirely to new social pressures, or it would completely resemble the place it was when it was opened. Furthermore, the school or college as a whole may be 'open' or 'closed', and individuals within the school will themselves be open or closed on various issues. For example, one teacher may be open to new ideas in teaching but closed to new ideas in social relations. One pupil may see vocational opportunities only in terms of his father's preferences, while another may be looking for quite exceptional ways of living his adult life. One department may be traditional in every regard while another is open to every whim and fashion.

It is difficult to conceive of a completely closed system. Human organizations which most nearly approach the completely closed type are prisons and mental hospitals, so far as most of the inmates are concerned. However, many people act as if a given organization is more 'closed' than outsiders would recognize. Schools are a case in point. Many schools, certainly in the past, have drawn boundaries around themselves so tightly as to keep even parents out. Rules have been made to regulate behaviour outside school hours, and the future world of pupils has been limited to those occupations the teachers considered desirable.

The effect of members behaving as if the school were a partially closed system is that they fail to observe the necessary exchanges with the environment that are required if the school is to keep in harmony with it. From a managerial point of view it is essential for an organization to collect information that will indicate future demands, and failure to recognize the validity of environmental relationships means that vital information cannot be obtained. Many schools were ill-prepared for secondary reorganization just because they failed to monitor the changes in educational and governmental attitudes that led to comprehensivization, for instance. In some schools teachers were psychologically unprepared for the change even though it had been declared local-authority policy for well over twenty years. Since in the case of most organizations members are also members of the environmental meta-systems there is usually more information available than they will actually import. One of the problems in organizational analysis is concerned with the way in which members do or do not perceive the relationship between their lives outside the organization and their lives inside. It is not uncommon for voluntary organizations to have budgeting problems, although there may be experienced financial experts among the members. On the other hand, some organizations make very great use of members' outside interests and gain increased vitality as a consequence. An examination of the use a school makes of a parents' association might be one way to indicate the extent to which that school operates as an open system. The over-all issue is the extent to which the school or college can utilize information that comes from its relationship with other bodies that share an interest in education.

Developing a Systems Model of the School

As we have seen, the basic ideas in a systems model are that organizations exist only in relationship to their larger environment. As a consequence they need to monitor their relationships. The process of monitoring involves gathering information and feeding it back into the system so that the system can change appropriately. An organization defines its relationship primarily in terms of goals, or transactional goals. Organizational effectiveness is measured by the ways in which an organization ensures that the goals are realistic and by the extent to which they are achieved.

Of course, the question of values arises because organizations (or rather members of organizations) have to select the information which they need and decide how to deal with it. At this juncture it is difficult to avoid value judgements since we all have preferences. For instance, poor examination results may lead to improved teaching or the abandonment of examinations altogether. The important thing is that dynamic systems consistently interact, and cope in a lively way both with the information they receive and the value conflicts among members.

Boundaries

Boundaries are material (economic, political, topographical), social and psychological. The boundary concept has been defined as follows: 'An organization has a boundary which separates it from its environment. Intakes cross this boundary and are subject to conversion processes within it. The work of the system is therefore, at least potentially, measurable by the difference between its intakes and its outputs.'[65] The boundaries may not be the same for every member of the organization, and even if they are notionally the same they may not have the same significance. Some colleges have difficulty in including laboratory staff in the same category as teaching staff – for instance, allowing the ancillary staff to use the common-room. Others cannot cope with adult evening students under the category of legitimate users. Some schools accept pupils as members during the day, but reject these same pupils when they attend the evening youth club. Many school-teachers see the school as a distinct economic and financial unit, while local education officers see each school as a member of a category that is subject to certain administrative formulae.

Psychological boundaries can be classified as emotional, temporal and physical. Membership within one type does not necessarily include membership within others. A pupil who day-dreams may have physical and temporal membership of the school but not emotional; his teachers find it impossible to bring him across this particular psychological boundary. Parents may be forbidden entry to the school building, yet they are psychologically present with their children, whose attitudes, values and behaviour are related more to their parents than the school. Alternatively a child at home may long so much for school-time that his play is devoted to things of the school. When schools fail to cross certain boundaries (for example into the wider activities of teachers' centres and curriculum development) many of their other activities are impaired.

Whatever boundaries exist, they are always permeable and need to be both crossed and controlled. The way in which organizations cross the boundaries is sometimes called the 'boundary-spanning function'. All the categories in an open-systems model require linking, and this function is often considered to be one of the major tasks of management. Although in most organizations the boundary-spanning function is formalized or institutionalized, it is a function of the organization rather than of individuals. That is to say that unless the function is performed, the organization will get into difficulties and someone will always perform the function by default. If a head is unable to relate to parents in the way they demand, other members of staff will be forced into surrogate positions. New and innovative schools have more boundary-spanning problems and opportunities than established ones. Good management must involve a conscious and deliberate exercising of boundary-spanning and boundary control, not to keep the boundaries closed but in order to ensure that they are appropriately permeable. Since no one individual can do this, boundary-spanning is an important area for delegation or sharing. Heads of small schools must realize that they should share this responsibility with their colleagues just as much as heads of large institutions. Being able to share in the boundary functions of an organization is a rewarding aspect of membership. Indeed, it is doubtful if membership can be considered to exclude boundary-crossing, since this activity is a measure of commitment, being a means of bringing environmental information into the organization and so adding to its chances of a healthy relationship with the larger system. The boundary of the school, for instance, is crossed when a teacher attends an Examination Board or a local-authority committee, and an internal boundary is crossed in a meeting between departments. Promotion or career paths often cross boundaries, as in the case of teachers assuming a pastoral role (in guidance or counselling), where they move from an academic to an administrative career path.

The Conversion Process

The central task (activity) of an organization, expressed in terms of a systems model, is the 'conversion process'. The conversion process is what goes on inside the institution related to the primary tasks. In most systems models, there seems to be an assumption that something is made or manufactured. However, in the case of organizations concerned almost entirely with people – schools, hospitals, prison, churches – the product idea becomes difficult to sustain. The idea of achievement may be useful in that purposeful activity is measured in terms of attainment, but there will be many forms of achievement, each measured by different criteria and according to different sets of values. For instance, schools may measure achievement of academic success by a number of quantitative criteria – percentage passes of entrants; percentage of certain grades; number of subjects compared with other schools, and so on. But almost certainly schools will be measuring other matters by other criteria – for example general literacy or good manners; jobs which former pupils obtain and the progress they make. In these latter cases the more important measures will be qualitative.

The Phenomenological Perspective: A Radical Alternative

3.8   . . . a mistaken belief in the reality of organizations has directed our attention from human action and intention as the stuff from which organizations are made. – T. Barr Greenfield

Greenfield in his article in *Reader 1* explains and argues the case for the phenomenological perspective as a radical alternative to the sort of 'objective' organization theory we have discussed so far. Activity 5 requires that you read the Greenfield piece. The article is a long one and Greenfield puts his case strongly. There are just three comments to be made here.

First, because Greenfield does not tell us very precisely, what is 'phenomenology'? In its broadest sense phenomenology is a descriptive philosophy of experience. In this century Edmund Husserl is the major exponent of this philosophy. However, it owes much to earlier work. Descartes, Leibniz, the British empiricists, Kant (who does get a mention from Greenfield), Brentano and James could all be said to have contributed something to it. As a philosophy of experience it is committed to rejecting all mention of anything beyond the possibilities of experience. Everything is to be questioned; all speculative constructions are to be rejected. All that can be admitted are perceptions and other experiences. Phenomenology is not a unified philosophical movement. At one extreme there are those phenomenologists who carry a large amount of metaphysical and mystical baggage – concepts of 'transcendence' and 'paratranscendence' are employed. At the other extreme (and this is closer to Greenfield's view) phenomenology can be regarded more as a methodology, with most of the idealist encumbrances shed. As Greenfield says, his 'alternative view' is 'a discipline for interpreting experience' and could therefore be applied, presumably as a kind of alternative, to other scientific methodologies. It is worth noting, however, that although, as Greenfield states, phenomenology has recently become more influential in British sociology and educational studies it has not made any great impact on academic *philosophy* as practised in universities in the UK.

Edmund Husserl

Greenfield seems to alternate between a strong and a weak thesis. Occasionally he seems to take a strong line – 'organizations are unreal . . . any attempt to understand them in terms of a single set of ideas, values and laws must be doomed to failure'. The weaker view emerges when you try to extract from his article some guides to action. These turn out to be ideas very similar to the human-relations view; for example, we should pay more attention to people in organizations, how they feel, think and act.

49

On pp. 60–1, Greenfield traces the connection between a view of organization theory–educational administration and the training of administrators or managers. 'Although the claim is seldom if ever made explicitly, this line of reasoning, linking a general theory of organization to the training of administrators, implies that we have at hand both the theory and the method which permits us to improve schools and the quality of whatever it is that goes on within them.' Actually, of course, as pointed out earlier in the unit, we do not have a single 'general theory' but a host of competing perspectives – including Greenfield's own. Greenfield, naturally enough, does not expound the criticisms which could be made of his theoretical position. Nor is there space in this unit to remedy this. If you are interested in following up some of the academic questions raised then you could start by reading the article by Hindess on 'The "phenomenological" sociology of Alfred Schutz'.[66]

Activity 5

Barr Greenfield reading

You should now read the Greenfield piece in *Reader 1*. It will be apparent why this is chosen as the concluding activity of this unit. You are not now being invited to choose between competing 'objective' theories; nor are you expected to synthesize a view from the 'objective' theories and schools of thought. Instead, you are being persuaded by Greenfield to forget 'objective' approaches and start anew from his radical 'alternative view'. To some extent this would be to stop at the end of Section 2 of this unit. Your task is to assess whether in fact general theories (note the plural) of organization have anything to offer the manager in education. Write a short critical review of the Greenfield article.

You should allow one hour for this Activity.

4 CONCLUSION

You developed in Section 2 a critical framework of your own perceptions and experience of schools as organizations. Then in Section 3 you critically reviewed several theoretical approaches to the subject. You should now be in possession of some kind of practical synthesis – a more or less integrated view of schools as organizations based on your own conceptions and the conceptions of others. It was left deliberately vague in the Introduction as to how this synthesis was to be formed. If you have worked hard and seriously through the unit the answer should now be clear. The method lies in practice, experience and reflection. This unit is merely a starting point.

NOTES

1   Fyfield, J. A. (1974) 'Theory for Practitioners: A Beginners' Course', *Journal of Educational Administration,* Vol. xii, no. 1, May 1974, pp. 45–8.

2   Etzioni, Amitai (1964) *Modern Organizations,* Englewood Cliffs, N. J., Prentice-Hall Inc., p. 1.

3   Hicks, H. G. (1967) *The Management of Organizations: A Systems and Human Resources Approach,* New York, McGraw-Hill (2nd edn. 1972), p. 4.

4   Cartwright, D. (1965) 'Influence, Leadership, Control' in March, J. G. (ed.) *Handbook of Organisations,* Chicago, Rand McNally, p. 1.

5   Silverman, D. (1970) *The Theory of Organizations,* London, Heinemann Educational, p. 8.

6   Hicks, H. G. (1967), op. cit., p. 23.

7   Silverman, D. (1970), op. cit., pp. 8–14.

8   Wittgenstein, L. (1963) *Philosophical Investigations,* Oxford, Basil Blackwell & Mott Ltd., p. 31.

9   Thomas, J. M. and Bennis, W. G. (eds.) (1972) *Management of Change and Conflict,* Harmondsworth, Penguin Books Ltd., p. 15.

10 Bittner, E. (1973) 'The School as a Formal Organization', in Salaman, G. and Thompson, K. (eds.) *People and Organizations,* London, Longman Group Ltd., p. 264.

11 From Etzioni, Amitai (1964), op. cit. (note 2), pp. 3–4.

12 Scott, W. R. (1964) 'Theory of Organizations', in Faris, R. E. L. (ed.) *Handbook of Modern Sociology,* Chicago, Rand McNally.

13 Perrow, C. (1974) 'Zoo Story' or 'Life in the Organizational Sandpit', Unit 15 of *People and Organizations,* Course D351, Milton Keynes, The Open University Press.

14 Dunkerley, D. (1972) *The Study of Organisations,* London, Routledge & Kegan Paul Ltd, pp. 56–67.

15 Bobbitt, H. R. et al. (1974) *Organizational Behaviour: Understanding and Prediction,* Englewood Cliffs, N. J., Prentice-Hall Inc., pp. 8–9.

16 Hoyle, Eric (1973) 'The Study of Schools as Organisations', in Houghton, Vincent, McHugh, Royston, and Morgan, Colin (eds.) (1975) *Management in Education Reader 1: The Management of Organizations and Individuals,* London, Ward Lock Educational/The Open University Press, Reading 2.2, p. 85.

17 Pugh, D. S. (1971) *Organization Theory,* Harmondsworth, Penguin Books Ltd., p. 9.

18 Pugh, op. cit., p. 99.

19 Davies, W. B. (1973) 'Organizational Analysis of Educational Institutions', in Brown, R. (ed.) *Knowledge, Education and Cultural Change,* London, Tavistock Publications Ltd., p. 254.

20 Davies, W. B., op. cit., p. 254.

21 March, J. G. (1974) 'Analytical Skills and the University Training of Educational Administrators', *Journal of Educational Administration,* Vol. xii, no. 1, May 1974.

22 March, op. cit., p. 24.

23 Willower, D. (1973) 'Schools, Values and Educational Inquiry', *Educational Administration Quarterly,* Spring 1973, Vol. ix, no. 2, p. 8.

24 March, op. cit. (note 21), p. 24.

25 Emery, T. E. and Trist, E. L. (1963) 'The Causal Texture of Organisational Environment', *Human Relations,* 18, August 1963, pp. 20–26.

26 Blau, P. M. and Scott, W. R. (1963) *Formal Organisations: A Comparative Approach,* London, Routledge & Kegan Paul Ltd., p. 51.

27 Davies, W. B. op. cit. (note 19), p. 259.

28 Willower, D., op. cit. (note 23), pp. 5–6.

29 Gribble, J. (1969) *Introduction to Philosophy of Education,* Boston, Allyn and Bacon, Chapter 1.

30 Harris, A. (1975) 'Decisions, Decisions . . .', in Dobson, Lance, Gear, Tony, and Westoby, Adam (eds.) (1975) *Management in Education Reader 2: Some Techniques and Systems,* London, Ward Lock Educational/The Open University Press, Reading 1.1.

31 Scheffler, I. (1973) *Reason and Teaching,* London, Routledge & Kegan Paul Ltd., p. 61.

32 March, op. cit. (note 21), pp. 24–5.

33 Davies, W. B., op. cit. (note 19), p. 253.

34 Hughes, M. G. (ed.) (1970) *Secondary School Administration: A Management Approach,* Oxford, Pergamon Press Ltd., p. 63.

35 Baron, G., and Taylor, W. (eds.) (1969) *Educational Administration and the Social Sciences,* London, University of London Athlone Press, pp. 112–13.

36 Simon, H. A. (1965) *The Shape of Automation,* New York, Harper & Row Publishers Inc., p. 58.

37 Davies, A. D. (1976) *The Teacher as Manager,* Maidenhead, McGraw-Hill Book Co. Ltd.

38 Lawrence, P. R. and Lorsch, J. W. (1967) *Organization and Environment,* Cambridge, Mass., Harvard University Press, pp. 161–3.

39 McGregor, Douglas (1967) *The Professional Manager,* New York, McGraw-Hill Book Co.

40 Oldham, Joyce (1975) 'Organizational Analysis in Education: An Empirical Study of a School', *Reader 1,* p. 368.

41 Miller, P. J. (1973) 'Factories, Monitorial Schools and Jeremy Bentham: The Origins of the "Management Syndrome" in Popular Education', *Journal of Educational Administration and History,* Vol. v, no. 2, July 1973, p. 10.

42 Crozier, M. (1972) 'Cultural Determinants of Organizational Behaviour' in Negandhi, A. R. (ed.) *Modern Organizational Theory,* Kent, Ohio, Kent State University Press, p. 219.

43 Bennett, S. J. (1974) *The School: An Organizational Analysis,* Glasgow, Blackie & Son Ltd., p. 85.

44 Bell, A. (1807) *Extract of a Sermon on the Education of the Poor,* London, W. Davies, p. 17.

45 Armytage, W. H. G. (1964) *Four Hundred Years of English Education,* Cambridge, Cambridge University Press, p. 90.

46 Bernard, Sir Thomas (ed.) (1809) *Of the Education of the Poor,* London, The Society for the Bettering of the Condition of the Poor, pp. 34, 36.

47 Callahan, R. E. (1962) *Education and the Cult of Efficiency,* Chicago, The University of Chicago Press.

48 Yee, A. H. (1972) 'The Limits of Scientific–Economic–Technological Approaches and the Search for Perspective in Education: The Case of Performance Contracting', *Journal of Educational Research,* Vol. 66, no. 1, September 1972, p. 19.

49 Massie, J. L. (1965) 'Management Theory', in March, J. G. (ed.) *Handbook of Organizations,* Chicago, Rand McNally. pp. 387–422.

50 Pugh, D. S. *et al.* (1971) *Writers on Organizations,* Harmondsworth, Penguin Books Ltd.

51 Owens, R. G. (1970) *Organizational Behavior in Schools,* Englewood Cliffs, N. J., Prentice-Hall Inc., p. 47.

52 Owens, op. cit., p. 47.

53 Perrow, C. (1972) *Complex Organizations,* Glenview, Ill., Scott, Foresman & Co., pp. 61–2.

54 Lupton, T. (1971) *Management and the Social Sciences,* Harmondsworth, Penguin Books Ltd., p. 35.

55 See Anderson, J. G. (1968) *Bureaucracy in Education,* Baltimore, Johns Hopkins Press, Chapter III, 'The Growth of Bureaucracy in the Schools'.

56 Bobbitt, H. R. *et al.* (1974) *Organizational Behaviour: Understanding and Prediction,* Englewood Cliffs, N. J., Prentice-Hall Inc., p. 64.

57 From Blau, P. M., and Scott, W. R. (1963) *Formal Organisations: A Comparative Approach,* London, Routledge & Kegan Paul Ltd., pp. 60.

58 Perrow, C., op. cit., (note 53); Anderson, J. G., op. cit., (note 55); Bidwell C. E. (1965) 'The School as a Formal Organization', in March, J. G. (ed.) *Handbook of Organizations,* Chicago, Rand McNally.

59 McGregor, Douglas (1960) *The Human Side of Enterprise,* New York, McGraw-Hill Book Co., pp. 33—57.

60 Strauss, G. (1969) 'Human Relations, 1968 Style', *Industrial Relations,* Vol. 7, no. 3, May 1969, pp. 262–76.

61 Selznick, P. (1970) *Law, Society and Individual Justice,* New York, Russell Sage Foundation.

62 Perrow, C. (1972), op. cit., (note 53), p. 142.

63 Owens, R. G. (1970), op. cit., (note 51), p. 48.

64 Argyris, Chris (1973) *Reader 1* Reading 3.5, p. 249.

65 Miller, E. J. and Rice, A. K. (1967) *Systems of Organization,* London Tavistock Publications Ltd.

66 Hindess, B. (1972) 'The Phenomenological Sociology of Alfred Schutz', *Economy and Society,* Vol. 1, no. 1.

ACKNOWLEDGEMENTS

Grateful acknowledgement is made to the following sources for material used in this unit:

Text

Extract from Amitai Etzioni, *Modern Organizations,* © 1964 Prentice-Hall Inc., Englewood Cliffs, New Jersey. Reprinted by permission.

Table

Table 2 from M. G. Hughes, *Secondary School Administration: A management approach,* Pergamon Press, 1970.

Figures

Figure 3 from S. J. Bennett, *The School: An organizational analysis,* Blackie, 1974; *Figure 4* adapted from R. G. Owens, *Organizational Behavior in Schools,* © Prentice-Hall Inc., Englewood Cliffs, New Jersey; *Figure 5* Griffith University, Brisbane; *Figures 7 and 8* from H. R. Bobbitt *et al., Organizational Behavior: understanding and prediction,* © 1974 Prentice-Hall Inc, Englewood Cliffs, New Jersey.
Reprinted by permission.

Illustrations

Portrait of F. W. Taylor The Bettman Archive Inc.; *Children in Sandpit* James Galt & Co. Ltd.; *Portraits of Edmund Husserl and Max Weber* Bildarchiv Preussischer Kultorbesitz; *The Registrar-General's Office* Mary Evans Picture Library; *Portrait of Margaret Maden* Camera Press, photograph by Tony McGrath.

MANAGEMENT IN EDUCATION

Management in Education: using the Literature